KATIE RIDDER

ROOMS

KATIE RIDDER

ROOMS

HEATHER SMITH MacISAAC

PRINCIPAL PHOTOGRAPHY BY ERIC PIASECKI

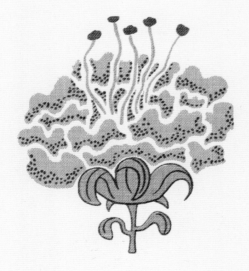

THE VENDOME PRESS

NEW YORK

Contents

Introduction

T'S TEMPTING TO THINK THAT THE open, sunny quality that infuses Katie Ridder's work has everything to do with her having grown up in California. But when other children were outside playing, Katie was happier to be indoors, working on any number of arts and crafts projects. By age twelve, she had her own quilting stand and was already selling cushion-size fabric fish and birds detailed with stitched scales and feathers at craft fairs. As a girl, she was thrilled to get a Singer sewing machine for her birthday. At fifteen, she redecorated her room, creating pillows and dust ruffles out of bold Marimekko sheets in a pale blue, white, and watermelon pattern of big tulips.

Craft is a hallmark of Katie's work. On every project she collaborates with master artisans who produce exquisite trims

Katie in the kitchen she designed for her parents when they lived in Woodside, California.

for curtains and upholstery, integrate antique textiles into pillows and ottomans, and embroider fancifully shaped headboards. They forge curtain rods and bedsteads, paint faux-bois doors, and fabricate fire screens or laser-cut panels or metal peony-blossom light fixtures or silk lanterns banded in velvet ribbon. Katie designs all of the above, produces her own line of fabrics and wallpapers, conceives and renews furniture via color and finish and hardware, and reimagines room surfaces (not just walls, but ceilings and floors as well) through the use of silver leaf, grasscloth, mirror, tile, one-of-a-kind stenciling, wallpaper, and simple paint.

For all the custom attention Katie lavishes on her interiors, they never project an air of "don't touch." Could it be that California emerges in the ease of her rooms? No matter how lavish a project, no matter its style and degree of sophistication, it remains accessible, family friendly, absolutely inviting, and subtly practical. A mother of three, Katie designs with real life in mind. Kitchen banquettes and coffee tables

OPPOSITE A woven Missoni cushion references the colors in a painting by Bill Jacklin and the Arts and Crafts–style linen wallcovering from Brunschwig & Fils. The camel side table is nineteenth-century Anglo-Indian.

are as durable as they are stylish, covered in chic fabrics like synthetic glazed linen or faux shagreen. Kids' rooms may feature unusual canopies and special chandeliers, but they also come equipped with trundle beds for sleepover pals and plenty of storage for toys, books, and personal collections.

In kitchens and bathrooms Katie deploys tile as a low-maintenance showstopper, transforming functional rooms into spaces flush with color and alive with reflected and refracted light. She treats tile not in a piecemeal fashion but as a decorative force. A Katie Ridder backsplash is no bit player.

New hanging lanterns from Anthropologie and ceramic lamps glazed in gold from Christopher Spitzmiller fit right into a recently restored early 1900s Japanese pavilion.

Nor is color. Amid a world of high-end interiors stuck in neutral, Katie's rooms beam in technicolor. Blues and greens have been favorites since the age of ten, when her childhood home was redone by local decorator Ann Valk. Witnessing the tufted sofas and crewelwork chairs, the looped carpets in geometric patterns, and the tones of blue and green all come together was seminal; it's when Katie decided she wanted to be a decorator, declaring so in writing for a school assignment.

To her preferred cool slice of the spectrum—peacock blue and turquoise, grass green and emerald—Katie added other, particularly tangy slices—orange, Chinese red, saffron, lemon—as her eye grew increasingly sophisticated. Matisse, her favorite artist, taught the art history major about color and shape and composition. As an editor at *House & Garden,* where she was exposed to the best decorators' work, she learned about fabrics and furniture plans, lighting and flowers, and the value of artisans. While at *House Beautiful,* she became adept at generating innovative ideas, mostly do-it-yourself projects involving paint or fabric, by doing them herself. As the owner of a decorating shop in the early nineties, she explored a newfound love of Turkish textiles, ceramics, tile, and metalwork that was groundbreaking at the time, winning over her first decorating clients with a fresh commingling of the traditional and the exotic.

Katie's interiors have the allure of a foreign accent amid American voices. Designs and motifs still uncommon in this country, like Islamic arches and Mughal-style flowers and leaves, appear consistently in her projects. Touches of Chinoiserie, splashes of Indian paisley and Provençal pattern, and stylized floral fabrics from Sweden converse with zebra rugs and geometric carpets. Tile work, like the overall application of zellige to broad surfaces in traditional Moroccan fashion, distinguishes her kitchens and bathrooms. The pattern-on-pattern, cheek-by-jowl mash-up of tile she witnessed in Istanbul's Topkapi Palace turns up in her layered treatment of texture and pattern, especially with textiles, from cushions to rugs. An entry hall light fixture is more likely to be

The faux-wood graining on the bedside table Katie designed for her bedroom sets off an antique bronze ornament.

a pierced brass lantern or an Asian-inspired silk globe than a crystal chandelier. Even the most traditional rooms feature something bright or bold or unorthodox or curious.

Underlying all the flair and panache are interiors that work as hard as Katie does. Behind every flourish is a solid reason for being. Rooms are not only pretty and welcoming, they are comfortable and thoughtful. Katie's interiors are open, both in the spaciousness of their plan and in their receptivity to new ideas. Air moves freely, unobstructed by heavy window treatments or clutter. For as cosmopolitan as Katie is in outlook, as distinct in color sense, she is at heart an American designer.

Entrances and Stair Halls

"More than a wow factor, I look for a delight factor when I design front halls."

KATIE RIDDER'S ENTRIES HAVE impact from the moment the front door swings open. The eye travels up to a stunning light fixture such as an antique crystal chandelier or a singular vintage light, a pierced brass lantern or a dramatic silk globe that she designed and had fabricated. On the wall may be a striking painting or a series of prints or a beautiful mirror, the latter both decorative and useful. Mirrors add light and sparkle, alter the perception of a space, and serve as a final checkup before you step out the door. The walls themselves may have been specially treated to a stenciled design or an exquisite wallpaper or a covering like grasscloth that not only adds visual dimension but is surprisingly practical. (Katie often specifies it for residences where strollers and bikes may be bumping into the walls.)

Underfoot, attention to design continues. Whether ebonizing or stenciling, tiling or furnishing with an unusual carpet, Katie treats the floor as another opportunity to add interest.

Entries don't usually require much furniture, but they do need to be *well* furnished. In decorating a transient space, form is more important than comfort. Chances are that a chair will only be used for a moment, as a place to remove shoes or park a bag, just as a table is a temporary resting place for keys and mail. Katie looks for chairs with unusual silhouettes and hall tables with graphic profiles. Or she might find (or make) a simple Parsons-style table in an unexpected material or color and layer it with lamps and other *objets*. She has placed Chinese altar tables, with their exotic fretwork and turned-in feet, in traditional settings and strictly modern tables in colonial entries. A console table of

In the generous foyer of an English Arts and Crafts–style house a French gilded-iron table, a pair of Persian inlaid rosewood chairs, and custom-made Viennese-inspired linen lanterns add a variety of form as well as an international flavor, elements found in nearly every foyer Katie decorates. Grasscloth-lined walls balance the deeper tones of the stained-wood floor and dimensional front door painted an unusual French violet.

any kind has the advantage of providing space beneath it for a stool or baskets to hold all sorts of things, from slippers to firewood to newspapers. No matter the style of table, flowers are likely to grace its surface, whether a lavish bouquet or an orchid with a single bloom.

Katie always provides for a living thing in her plan for the entrance hall. In addition to contributing a lovely scent, flowers or a plant project an air of freshness, growth, and nurture. She loves fresh-cut branches—flowering in spring, dotted with berries in fall—for their height and variety. Plants such as a topiary or a potted palm lend the room presence, not unlike a singular chair. Even the suggestion of something organic, like a painted wall treatment of vines, does the trick.

Just because stair halls and hallways are spaces we pass through doesn't mean they shouldn't be memorable. They deserve as much decorative attention as any other space. Long halls in particular present challenges. Katie animates them by using small groupings of furniture to create distinct areas. A composition as simple as a chair, a picture, and a sconce provides a place to physically—or just

Every Entry Needs:

- A welcoming light such as an iron-and-glass lantern
- An exterior doormat made of rubber, along with a bootscraper in harsh climates
- An interior doormat, preferably a rectangle of coco set into the floor
- An interesting floor, such as one of stenciled wood, or an antique carpet
- A coat closet equipped with wood hangers, lower hooks or cubbies for kids' coats and gear, shelves for hats, and trays for wet boots
- An umbrella stand
- A table or shelf for mail, keys, and miscellany
- A combination of overall lighting (an unusual chandelier) and welcoming lighting (a table lamp with a detailed shade)

visually—pause. Lamps on tables are always good in halls; they create warm pools of light that draw the eye. Picture lights over artwork have the same effect in hallways too narrow for furniture. And because halls often need all the light they can get, Katie is in favor of windows unobstructed by curtains or blinds.

Still, given a chance to embellish, Katie usually takes it, lining halls with wallpaper, antique runners, and collections of prints, elevating plain doors with faux-bois painting, adding pretty hardware to doors and trim to custom-made silk shades in exotic shapes. But ever practical, she also considers the wear and tear halls are subjected to. Whenever possible, she recesses a rectangle in the floor just inside the front door to accommodate a coco mat that can be swapped out when it's too worn. Likewise, wood wainscoting is a decorative and durable wall covering for entries, especially mudrooms, just as tile floors are ideal for vestibules. Stair runners are long-wearing wool broadloom in medium to dark tones, often with a stripe or subtle small pattern that disguises dirt and footprints. For Katie, no aspect of a hall is an afterthought, even though it's a space often overlooked.

What was once a breezeway is now a bright and welcoming entry to a coastal California house. A coat of taupe paint unites architectural elements while wavy tile in varied blue glazes, a nod to the nearby ocean, has replaced a wood floor. Prints of tropical birds, pieces of coral, a giant shell, a potted orchid, and a pierced-brass Moroccan lantern maintain the connection to the out-of-doors. This room demonstrates that an entry can be both sparsely furnished and beautifully decorated when all of its surfaces are considered.

LEFT The back hall of a house in Arkansas receives every bit as much attention as the entry. The oriental rug, custom three-pillow ottomans, aubergine-painted molding, reproduction English Arts and Crafts wallpaper, and even the velvet ribbon trimming the lampshades reflect the client's love of lavender. The antique Italian console table supports an outsize pair of American mid-century wooden lamps.

OPPOSITE With its classical sconces, eccentric French chandelier, antique painted Swedish settee, and diamond-patterned seagrass rug, the entry of a mid-century California house strikes a comfortable balance between formal and informal. An oval landscape painting hung opposite the front door is reflected in the chandelier's pendant convex mirror.

OPPOSITE Touches of red appear throughout this Park Avenue apartment. Here, in the entry, a Parsons table lacquered Chinese red, the fabric of a custom sofa, and coral drops hanging from a pair of oversize custom light fixtures spice neutral grasscloth walls trimmed in glossy chocolate brown.

ABOVE In an octagonal New York apartment foyer, the graceful lines of an ebonized settee once owned by the Duchess of Windsor, reupholstered in inky blue horsehair, echo the curves of a painting by Caio Fonseca. Like a piece of jewelry, a chandelier of gilded metal and Austrian crystals adds sparkle.

ABOVE LEFT An oval gilded English mirror picks up on the sinuous legs of a French hall table from the 1940s. A piece of ornamental bronze work by Antonio Gaudí covers the peephole of the faux-bois-painted front door.

ABOVE RIGHT A series of white squares painted atop an ebonized floor lend rhythm and graphic definition to a long, gallery-like hall uniting two formerly separate apartments. In contrast, the furnishings display curves.

OPPOSITE The tiny elevator vestibule is animated by tendril-like wall stencils, taken from a book and exploded in scale, and the swirling pattern of the unexpected yet practical mosaic floor.

OPPOSITE An enormous tole lantern and a fine marble-topped Regency table support the grandeur of a stair hall in a nineteenth-century Italianate house in Virginia horse country. The warm hues of the Zuber wallpaper and the antique Oushak carpet reference the colors of autumn hunting season, when the house is most used.

RIGHT A Chinese altar table and walls stenciled in a Japanese woodblock motif that was found in a magazine and enlarged add exotic notes to a traditional stair hall in a New York apartment. As in all her foyers, Katie seeks out or creates distinctive light fixtures. Here, orange silk globes, inspired by Josef Hoffmann fixtures at the Neue Galerie in New York City, counter the otherwise cool palette.

In the gracious front hall of a grand Italianate house, the natural woods of fine antique furnishings complement the warm wall and floor colors. A variety of metal accents—wall sconces, hanging lantern, brass pulls on the tall chest, inlaid pedestal of the central table, gilded legs of the console table—add a subtle glow.

ABOVE Against the white-painted wood walls in the stair hall of a house on Nantucket, the simple lines of the handrail and an antique brass sconce stand out. The soft blue accent color brings to mind the ocean.

OPPOSITE A collection of antique embroideries of seascapes hung in asymmetrical groupings offsets the formality of the traditional stair. The shape of the iron chandelier mirrors the hand-painted compass rose below it.

OPPOSITE A wall of Damien Hirst spin paintings framed in white extends the architecture of a stairwell's wall of windows. The bright striped carpet picks up the colors in the paintings, while the vintage chandelier echoes their circular motif.

ABOVE The double doors of a town-house open into an entry hall packed with unexpected drama. Chinese red trim picks up the palette of Katie's own "Pagoda" wallpaper. A silk light fixture four times the size of the French antique that inspired it casts a glow on the gold-leaf ceiling and populates the tall, narrow space.

OVERLEAF, LEFT AND RIGHT In Katie's own entry hall, a coco mat is set into the original marble floor just inside the front door. A Khotan rug from Turkestan introduces a tree theme that is picked up in the bronze faux-bois table base and free-form custom stone top. A handrail of candy red and silver leaf dresses up a Queen Anne balustrade.

Living Rooms

"A living room should be as enticing a place to read a book as it is to entertain.
The room must have more than one use."

A SUCCESSFUL LIVING ROOM beckons you to explore, then invites you to stay awhile. Less a product of decoration than sensibility, it projects an understated confidence that infuses its furnishings and puts guests at ease. Such are Katie's living rooms; in spite of every element being given great consideration, the atmosphere is one of relaxed hospitality. If "decorating is not a look but a point of view," in the words of legendary practitioner Albert Hadley, then Katie's guiding principle is: you're only going to have a good time in your living room if it's a place you want to be.

Of course, a lot goes into making a living room have ease. Katie always starts with a furniture plan. After interviewing her clients about decorating styles, furnishings they may already have that they wish her to incorporate, and how they will use the room, she works up two alternate schemes to present. The styles and palette may vary but the organization of the plan remains the same. No matter the size of a living room, it needs discrete and intimate seating areas, each furnished with comfortable places to sit, tables to place things on, and suitable lighting.

A furniture plan establishes a game plan. Even for the amateur, working one out is a good exercise because, as every professional decorator knows, a plan answers a lot of questions, saving time and money. A successful furniture plan strikes a balance in size, scale, style, and form. The goal is a combination of open areas and intimate clusters, of furniture that is predominantly about volume, like an upholstered

In a San Francisco house, traditional furnishings in subtle shades like a club chair in distressed linen velvet, a Knole sofa, and an Oushak carpet allow a bold painting by James Brooks to take center stage. With its mix of brass, wood, bamboo, bronze, leather, ceramic, and all kinds of fabrics, this living room exemplifies a key element of Katie's rooms: they always feature an eclectic array of materials.

Bright furnishings—a wing chair inspired by a William III model and upholstered in yellow linen, curtains in a printed silk from Sweden, green grasscloth on the walls, a triple-weave Beauvais carpet in yellow and sand, and a foo dog that once belonged to Katie's great-uncle—reflect the casual golf course setting of this California house. In her choice of textiles, Katie democratically and routinely stirs up a blend of stylized florals, geometrics, and solids.

sofa, and pieces that are open frames, like tables and wooden side chairs. Ideally, you want a pleasing mix of skirted upholstery and pieces with exposed legs.

You also want graphic variety (solid with pattern) and layers of texture, which can be achieved with fabrics, by mixing materials (wood, metal, leather, ceramic), and by playing with finish (smooth, hammered, limed, gilded, ebonized, mirrored). Katie's sofas tend to be of a solid color accented with toss pillows that are covered in a mix of new and antique textiles. The more neutral the sofa, the more lively the coffee table and vice versa. Since coffee tables generous in size and impervious to drinks and other wear are hard to come by, Katie often designs her own. A favorite is a Parsons-style table wrapped in a synthetic fabric that adeptly mocks the authentic material. For a faux-shagreen table, she had the yardage cut and pieced to read all the more like the real thing. The result: a chic and nearly indestructible coffee table.

Nothing does more to pull a living room together and set off a variety of furniture than a beautiful carpet. Katie likes them large, stopping less than a foot shy of the walls, and patterned. Antique Oushaks populate more formal living rooms (budgets permitting). Their colors are luminous, their designs subtle, and their pile just the right degree of plush. But Katie is equally pleased with the effect of wool broadloom in graphic patterns both bold and discreet, as well as with traditional hooked rugs in contemporary stripes for country and historic settings. Reversible triple-weave carpets have

Anatomy of a Full-Length Curtain

- ◆ **Overall style:** simple rod and rings in bronze or black finish (Katie has custom rods made by Morgik)
- ◆ **Curtain style:** French pleat, pinched at the top
- ◆ **Fabrics:**
  - ◇ wool felt
  - ◇ wool sateen, because it hangs beautifully and takes embroidery well
  - ◇ printed linen for its texture, variety of pattern, and more casual feel
- ◆ **Trims:** Contrasting trim to call out the leading edge

the advantage of changing the look of a room with just the flip of a rug.

A rug that's large but not wall-to-wall has the advantage of pulling the furniture away from its typical default position—hugging the perimeter. Instead, the rug gives the room a field in which to "float" furniture. Even an antique rug never stops Katie from placing a sitting area in the middle of the room. Since the carpet has likely been repaired multiple times already, she thinks nothing of cutting a small slit in it (which can later be sewn closed) to accommodate wiring. Katie regularly installs electrical outlets in living room floors, thereby freeing table and floor lamps to cozy up to sofas and reading chairs. Yet another reason for a well-thought-out furniture plan.

With the furniture established, Katie then spices a room with glints of metal and flashes of color. Because lamps come in so many different hard (base) and soft (shade) materials, they are an easy way to achieve diversity. Their variety of form and size also facilitates mixing it up. In a single living room, Katie may combine bronze floor lamps with turned-wood buffet lamps, ceramic table lamps, and a crystal chandelier. Every living room needs not only many light sources but a variety of intensities of light, from bright for reading to softer for atmosphere. What's more inviting than a room with multiple warm pools of light? Like lamps, accessories such as vases and other vessels, boxes, sculpture, books, and natural objects such as shells provide a variety of form and color and serve as destinations for the eye.

PRECEDING PAGES A German Baroque secretary and Julian Schnabel's tribute to Anna Magnani (an artist's proof) add vertical elements of striking contrast in Katie's own living room. She embellished the club chairs with a woven tape in a butterscotch color and pillows from John Stefanidis. Between the chairs is a tile-topped French table from the 1960s; behind them, a late-eighteenth-century console table from Finland.

OPPOSITE A 1910 Persian carpet drove the palette of blue and camel in Katie's living room. The hand-painted trim of the beige wool sateen curtains and the pillows of vintage textiles and trims pick up the cobalt blue in the rug. The English nineteenth-century mirror used to hang above the fireplace in Katie's childhood home; the American settee was her great-grandmother's.

ABOVE Slipper chairs upholstered in peacock blue wool felt add a modern note to the classically detailed room. The low Chinese-style coffee table, painted orange by Katie, references the Chinese watercolor of Hong Kong harbor above the fireplace.

Lavender walls with a pearlized finish are the luminous foil for a painting by Jacqueline Humphries above a custom sofa. Katie derived its unusual shape from a piano. The ottoman features an antique textile from Virginia Di Scascio, a longtime favorite source.

In addition to hiding an unsightly radiator, a custom L-shaped sofa
of limed oak and mohair makes the most of limited wall space.
Pillow covers in a variety of antique textiles and a geometric
Beauvais carpet enliven the solid colors of the upholstered pieces,
while the amoeba-shaped coffee table lends an element of fun.
Katie's rooms always strike a balance between plain and fanciful,
extravagant and practical.

Floating a sofa in front of a window provides a great place to read in natural light. Here the window backlights the strong silhouette of a sofa whose curves are further highlighted by contrast welting. Curtains accented with a woven trim, a coffee table covered in faux shagreen, and a club chair upholstered in "Contessa" from Home Couture add color and texture. Katie tends to prefer minimal curtain hardware, but her curtains themselves are almost always embellished with trim.

ABOVE A Parsons table in bone-colored lacquer serves as both a decorative table and a minimal desk in a city apartment living room. Placing it in front of the window takes advantage of the high-rise view.

RIGHT Venetian-glass floor lamps frame a custom sofa that tucks into one corner, wrapping around a coffee table covered in melon-colored faux sharkskin. Katie modeled the boldly striped, three-cushion ottoman on a Turkish example.

The living room of a house in Southampton, NY, feels summery yet substantial, with a whiff of the exotic. Reproduction Art Deco chairs in a cabana stripe flank a custom ottoman with an antique French textile wrapping the base. An antique Swedish caned bench and an inlaid Indian table have a similar delicacy. Like the strié-patterned cotton fabric on the sofa, the blue linen curtains, bordered in an embroidered wave, reference the nearby ocean.

OPPOSITE In a room lined with overflowing bookcases, the furnishings of a summer house are intentionally light and easy. A chair in a chrysanthemum print and a striped ottoman add colorful punch; a rope chair and a brass wire light fixture add texture.

ABOVE Chartreuse leather brightens a pair of English ebonized fireside chairs. Roman shades in a subtly figured fabric from John Stefanidis pick up on the watered-down green-yellow hue of the walls.

RIGHT Running bookcases floor to ceiling transforms them from furniture into architecture. In this coastal California living room, the hundreds of books on display not only are easily retrievable but also serve as intriguing "wallpaper." Against such a mix of texture and color, a voluptuous sofa stands out, especially in bright watery blue.

OVERLEAF A generous living room facing San Francisco Bay features three distinct seating areas as well as a quatrefoil-shaped ottoman in front of a seventeenth-century French mantelpiece. Pale green curtains crowned by a crenellated pelmet and chairs upholstered in soft moss and olive offset the warm stucco walls, antique Oushak carpet, and Renaissance-style wooden ceiling, to which Katie added multicolored stenciling with gold highlights.

LEFT Chinese lacquered cupboards, a pair of garden stools in a similar glossy red, and cushions in printed linen add a touch of the exotic to a traditionally paneled room painted a pale celadon.

ABOVE A banquette of strié-patterned velvet detailed with nailheads turns a bay window into an intimate seating area illuminated by a trio of beaded lights.

ABOVE A sofa and club chair upholstered in light solid colors and a coffee table covered in pale shagreen balance the rich textures of a Coromandel screen and an Axminster rug.

OPPOSITE A sofa in orange linen and twin poufs in red and orange antique silk pick up the colors in the rug while a pair of chairs recovered in a Robert Kime linen play off its pattern.

PRECEDING PAGES The calm, symmetrical arrangement of chairs upholstered in quiet seafoam ultrasuede ensures that nothing competes with a beautiful panoramic view of Nantucket. Curtains of hand-blocked linen, embroidered pillows, and an ottoman accented with antique textiles add a balanced layer of pattern.

OPPOSITE References to a Nantucket house's island location are subtly nautical: teak chairs brightened by a printed cotton, brass tables, a model of a barque, and hurricane lamps.

ABOVE A linen sofa defines different seating areas of a Nantucket living room, its lavender hue an inspired departure from watery blues.

OPPOSITE The profile of an antique Swedish bench reads like ocean waves, especially set before a window looking out to the water. A bobbin stool lends additional dimension to the flat curves of the bench.

ABOVE The bright stripes of a handmade hooked rug pick up the colors in a series of paintings by Carl Palazzoo. Behind a coffee table of lacquered linen, an antique textile from the client's own collection, sewn onto the back of the sofa, reduces its mass.

A bright blue Shaker barrel used as a side table, a vintage enamel pitcher, an ottoman of tomato-colored glazed synthetic raffia, and a pair of chairs in cotton embroidered with big blue flowers bring cheerful primary notes to an otherwise subtle palette. For less formal rooms, Katie often turns to geometrically patterned carpets like this striped wool rug.

ABOVE Fabric patterns play off each other in a Rhode Island summer house: geometric on the side chairs, a larger-scaled stripe for the substantial sofa, and an overall floral for the curtains.

OPPOSITE The small tassels on a curtain's leading edge pick up the rhythm of the horizontal stripes. The pattern of the sofa fabric is a floral, a geometric, and a stripe rolled into one.

OPPOSITE De Gournay wallpaper, custom figured and colored for an Arkansas living room, ties together furnishings as disparate as a coral-colored Macao garden seat, lavender Murano glass lamps, an antique Swedish clock, and an oak table in the manner of Pugin.

ABOVE Glazed linen curtains in a shade of hyacinth and a yellow-skirted club chair accented with blue-gray banding and nailheads flank a custom corner sofa à la Jean-Michel Frank.

OVERLEAF Books and exotic objects—a Victorian marble specimen mirror, a shell-encrusted box, a faience platter, an Anglo-Raj quill box, and a piece of coral—top an English tiered table.

The Country Houses of DAVID ADLER

ACANTHUS PRESS

PRECEDING PAGES Katie had an antique gilded-wood valance in the shape of branches reproduced for all the parlor windows of a grand Virginia house, then commissioned Penn & Fletcher to embroider berries, twigs, and leaves on mossy green wool sateen for the pelmet and curtains. Damask covers a pair of tufted club chairs; the ebonized and gilded English chairs retain their original leather upholstery.

LEFT Bronze bookcases and curtain rods, furniture in dark woods like walnut, and gridded-metal light fixtures add line and form to the soft, pale palette of an airy New York living room.

ABOVE An Indian coffee table and a Raj chair pull up to a sofa that's a copy of an English antique. The curtains are printed linen from Galbraith & Paul.

LEFT Linen sofas flank a two-tone Lucite coffee table in a Hamptons living room. Katie concocted the painted wall lozenges on site, deriving their colors from the pillow textiles. A Josef Frank print covers the chair and ottoman.

OVERLEAF Sisal carpet, unlined linen curtains, and cotton ticking cushions for a painted bench suit the casual air of a summer house. Katie had the wooden tables made, then painted them a medium blue-gray.

THE HAMPTONS KEN MILLER

The Peggy Guggenheim Collection of Modern Art

EARTH FROM ABOVE

ABOVE Curtains of blue stitching on a faille-like white silk by Jennifer Robbins Textiles frame a view of Central Park. The embroidered velvet on the spoon chairs picks up the green of the trees.

RIGHT Katie chose a "starry-night blue" to highlight the predominantly gold antique screen. The brown linen sofa is detailed with Fortuny panels and a woven tape.

OPPOSITE AND RIGHT
In a round of SWAT decorating, Katie bought everything—vintage furniture, ponyskin rugs, Bagues chandeliers, even dishes and towels—for this Buenos Aires apartment locally and installed it all in a week. By painting the steel staircase red, she turned an element with overbearing presence into a more intriguing and sculptural room divider.

OVERLEAF, LEFT A bureau found at a flea market is now, with a fresh coat of teal blue, a television stand.

OVERLEAF, RIGHT
A sheepskin-covered bench and a mid-century sofa flank an antique carpet laid atop a larger sisal rug.

Studies and
Family Rooms

"Family rooms should invite gathering and stand up to the accumulations that come with an active life."

ASIDE FROM KITCHENS, studies and family rooms are the most favored, well-used rooms in the house. Like kitchens, they are informal spaces where everyone gathers for communal activities like playing games and watching movies. Yet they are also rooms in which one feels at ease being alone: reading in a comfy chair, working at the computer, delving into a craft project. To be all things to all users, of all ages and inclinations, these rooms must have one thing guiding their design: flexibility.

From cozy and colorful to spacious and bright, Katie's studies and family rooms are inviting yet always hardworking spaces. So often are her studies and home offices lined with bookshelves that they have the look of cheerful libraries. Katie turns to bookcases not only to provide necessary storage and lend a room character but also to literally shape the space. Bookcases built perpendicular to a wall create reading nooks; those built out around a window frame it in an alcove and provide a deep sill or window seat. They almost always reach to the ceiling, thereby graduating from the supporting role of furniture to that of a lead player in the room's architecture. Katie, in fact, uses bookcases to disguise architectural irregularities as well as to play down equipment like televisions and sound systems by building it in. Other unsightly paraphernalia of modern life (printers, tech equipment, and office files) is tucked away in cabinets incorporated into the base of the bookcases.

Unlike most book-lined studies, which tend to be sober affairs, Katie's are alive with color. Often a single vibrant hue will unite bookcases, window frames, doors, baseboards, and

In an Arkansas sitting room, bookcases form a reading nook for a sofa, and an oak English Arts and Crafts table serves as both library and craft table. Chinese-inspired embroidery spills over the folds of the silk roman shade. Katie likes brass wall sconces for their space-saving flexibility, directed light, and touch of luster.

crown moldings. The envelope of color visually organizes the diversity that books bring to a room. All sorts of wall-mounted lighting, from adjustable sconces for reading to fixed sconces and picture lights attached directly to the bookcases, provide pockets of illumination that turn a room bright by day into a cozy hideaway at night.

Color begets color in Katie's studies and family rooms. For furnishings to hold their own against a backdrop of a strong hue, they must have strength in form, boldness of pattern, or some other mark of distinction. Sofas and club chairs are not just deep and comfortable; they're also bright conversationalists. Solid-colored upholstery is still bold, frequently dressed up with contrast trim, and always layered with toss pillows in lively textiles. Desks, tables, and side chairs, like one from India inlaid with mother-of-pearl are chosen for their unique silhouettes or unusual finishes. Like couture costume jewelry, lamps and hanging fixtures in unusual shapes and sizes accessorize the room with flair. Never one to miss an opportunity to elevate the ordinary, Katie trims plain lampshades with ribbon and replaces nondescript finials with accents like coral branches.

For all the decorative panache on display, Katie's studies and family rooms are grounded in practicality, starting with

The Best Bookcase:

- Is built in and reaches to the ceiling to provide instant architecture
- Has shelves 12" deep, the optimum for a mix of books and objects
- Has an exposed shelf edge a minimum 1½" thick, especially if the shelf is wide, for good support and visual substance
- Has cabinetry at the base to provide storage or hide a radiator
- Is painted the same color as the trim and even the walls of the room
- Has its own lighting in the form of sconces or picture lights

the floor coverings. Broadloom carpet in patterns ranging from optical to tilelike to zebra to regular stripes is hard wearing and hides a host of sins. As do upholstery fabrics like mohair, linen, cotton duck, and leather. Katie frequently opts to line the walls of family rooms with grasscloth or fabrics that, in addition to contributing pattern and texture, are surprisingly durable. Roman shades, both more casual and less expensive than formal window treatments, still provide an additional canvas for pattern and color.

Small-scaled furnishings like leather poofs and ceramic garden stools allow for a flexible furniture arrangement, inviting kids as well as grownups to participate in customizing a space. Tables positioned away from the wall to accommodate chairs to either side do double duty as desks and casual, intimate dining areas. Lower tables and ottomans are good for games and snacks when everyone prefers to sprawl on the floor. Decorative baskets and boxes organize toys, remote controls, and office and school supplies. Though Katie provides a place for everything, her studies and family rooms are far from static. Quite the opposite: loaded with both charm and good sense, they are friendly hosts, good working partners, and easy companions.

Comfortable reading chairs reupholstered in yellow leather are the color wheel complement to walls soaked in Farrow & Ball's Ballroom Blue. Katie frequently balances cool hues with warm tones or lifts quieter palettes with bright colors. The textured surface of the brass giraffes mimics the circles in the contemporary print.

OPPOSITE Chairs reuphol-
stered in wool melton
accented with a woven tape
flank a japanned keyhole desk.
Two tones of butterscotch in
plush and flat pile produce a
mazelike pattern in the carpet.

RIGHT A pillow fashioned
from a piece of an antique
kimono adds a dash of color
to a sofa in strié-patterned
mohair. Adjustable brass
sconces, a gilded French
table from the 1950s, and
brass nailheads contribute
accents of gold.

OPPOSITE Marbleized paper lines the back of bookshelves that are painted the same glossy coral as the trim and under-window cabinets. The burnished leather of vintage chairs picks up the warm hue.

ABOVE Lavender panels of leather set into strips of painted wood lend a distinctive air to a small study carved out of a former passageway. Katie plays the natural pattern of the zebra carpeting off the grid of the walls.

A study where a jewelry designer meets with clients is lined with elegant leather walls and studded with fine furnishings. An early-twentieth-century French brass lamp sits on an unusual Chinoiserie desk inlaid with bone. Brass sconces with silk shades light red velvet sofas that were modeled after antiques Katie saw in Paris.

OPPOSITE In the library of Katie's house, original woodwork rubbed with linseed oil sets off a collection of photos, paintings, and etchings of classical images and scenes of New York. A pair of antique French stools upholstered in white pony hide flank a cast-iron tile-topped table from the Paris flea market.

ABOVE A Suzani tapestry panel set into the pink silk velvet sofa, which Katie designed, picks up where the tilelike pattern of the flat-weave carpet leaves off. She painted the arched niche red to highlight a bronze sculpture, *Scholar's Rock*, and silvered the ceiling to subtly extend the daylight from wraparound windows.

OPPOSITE In a Connecticut sunroom early-twentieth-century oak tables in the Moorish style flank a sofa Katie copied from an antique and covered in an orange indoor/outdoor fabric by Pollack. Glazed calfskin tops a hexagonal ottoman wrapped in a fabric from Vanderhurd.

RIGHT Brilliant colors, a zebra-hide rug, and a Lucite coffee table punch up a traditional study. A Jansen-style chair covered in "Chiang Mai Dragon" from Schumacher pulls together Chinese blue walls and a sofa in red mohair from John Hutton called "Happy Hour."

ABOVE LEFT A trio of mercury-glass teardrop vases atop an animal-leg table painted blue bounces sunlight around a solarium in Arkansas.

ABOVE RIGHT Painted caned chairs and a glazed-linen coffee table reinforce the summery feel of the room, while a red sofa anchors the seating arrangement.

OPPOSITE Cool and smooth Moroccan cement tiles "carpet" the floor in pattern. Caning, tufting, a frond floor lamp, and ikat and batik pillows add texture.

ABOVE A fifteen-foot sofa had to be built in place in Katie's ZamZam, aka family room, formerly service rooms over the garage. The sofa is perfect for sleepovers, as are easily rearranged leather poufs, low tables, and Herman Miller chairs with bright red cotton webbing. Katie's sofas always feature pillows in a variety of sizes, shapes and textiles.

OPPOSITE An Indian fabric panel Katie found in Paris frames the door to the family room and sets the stage for the red, blue, and yellow palette captured in a Moroccan rug laid over striped wool carpeting. The fire breast was first mirrored and then layered with Morroccan mosharabi lattice panels.

LEFT The window wall of a New York family room was moved forward to create a bookcase and deep sills and hide a radiator. Katie updated an existing sofa by removing its skirt, converting multiple cushions into one long one, and reupholstering it in a hard-wearing blue boiled wool trimmed in green moss fringe.

ABOVE Beetle Cat sailboats on wallpaper designed by Katie circle a Nantucket playroom above open shelving designed to hold games. The striped wool rug stops just shy of the baseboard, exposing the hardwood floor and avoiding a wall-to-wall look.

ABOVE Blue appliqués and blue silk cushions embellish a brown linen sofa in a New York sitting room. Silk shades in an exotic shape top lamps of tobacco-colored glass. Unlined silk velvet curtains in a creamy red add a soft warmth.

OPPOSITE An American desk from the 1950s, an Anglo-Indian chair, and an armoire to house a computer printer and supplies form a chic home office in a corner of a New York sitting room. Behind a sofa upholstered in olive cut velvet, wooden blinds in concert with wool sateen curtains admit light while hiding a nearby building.

ABOVE A home office/TV room in Rhode Island picks up the same apple green—on window frames, in the leather of the Eames desk chair, in the cotton rug—as that used in the adjacent kitchen (see page 163). The windows remain intentionally bare of treatments that could trap cooking smells.

OPPOSITE Plantation shutters disguise sliding glass doors in a sitting room lined with a checkerboard of horizontal and vertical grasscloth. A desk doubles as a sofa table, supporting lamps to light the seating area. The flat fire screen trimmed in bronze strips was designed by Katie.

OPPOSITE Nautical paintings, a basket-based lamp, and colorful pillows on the linen sofa lend an informal summery feel to a family room in Rhode Island. The oversize leather-topped ottoman with a built-in shelf for books and games is a perfect practical multipurpose centerpiece.

ABOVE An all-over coat of turquoise paint unites walls, trim, bookcases, and cabinets. Stacked rush baskets hold children's toys. An Asian desk and chair and blue-and-white porcelain ginger jars atop the bookcase contribute a foreign accent to an American room

ABOVE Glossy olive paint defines a bar area between the library and the solarium of a house in Arkansas. Shelving of nickel and glass fairly disappears against the silver-on-peacock Japanese Floral wallpaper by Florence Broadhurst lining the niche.

RIGHT In addition to contributing glamour, a studded grid of brass nailheads atop red leather breaks up the expanse of the long walls of a basement family room in San Francisco. The tole table and chairs and the French postal desk came from the Paris flea market.

OPPOSITE Katie updated a historic Japanese pavilion by adding reproduction Chinese tables, Moroccan lamps, a Beckley mattress on a new sofa base, green silk curtains, and a simple paper lantern to the sitting area.

ABOVE An antique Moroccan rug comfortably coexists with a japanned mirrored dresser, part of a suite of furniture original to the pavilion. Wall murals featuring geese and bamboo were restored.

ABOVE A pair of mirrors over striped banquettes multiplies the windowed doors that slide into the walls of a pool pavilion in Virginia. Cane-backed mahogany chairs with cushions in a crisp Lulu DK printed cotton are light and elegant.

RIGHT Aside from fantastical coquillage chandeliers and sconces by British artist Belinda Eade, the furniture of the pool pavilion is eminently practical; indoor/outdoor fabric in bright red and blue covers all of the upholstered pieces.

Dining Rooms

"I want my dining rooms to present an enticing view all the time.
They should shine year 'round."

COLOR PLAYS A ROLE IN EVERY room Katie touches, but in her dining rooms it is the star. Not only does she set a dramatic stage for the players around a dining table and for the feast itself, but she creates a space that's alluring even when not in use. Too often the dining room in American homes is regarded as little more than a container for a table and chairs to be dressed up for holidays and other significant occasions. All the more reason to shower attention on it, as Katie does, transforming it from the runt of the litter into best in show.

Dining rooms typically come to life in the evening, when the lights are low and candles are lit. During the day, they are rooms we mostly pass by or glimpse from another. For that very reason they can handle color—and lots of it. Katie loves to experiment with far more saturated hues in dining rooms, in everything from paint surfaces to curtain fabrics to upholstery, lighting, accessories, and flowers. Because her clients often ask her to outfit a dining room from soup to nuts, her color choices can extend even to tabletop items, right down to the napkin rings.

In breaking the dining room out of its typical torpor, Katie not only pumps up the color but frees furnishings from the stranglehold of too much brown wood. Rarely does a dining room she designs have more than one major piece of furniture in natural wood. The dining table is the most likely candidate, or maybe a sideboard. But hardly ever are the table and chairs in the same wood, unless they are valuable antiques or family heirlooms. Even then she will work to take the traditional pieces out of context by, for instance,

An Arkansas dining room captures devices Katie uses to invigorate an often-overlooked room: strong color, two-tone chairs (solid meets pattern), an unusual light fixture, and a dash of sparkle. Chairs upholstered in claret mohair and lavender and white China Seas cotton joined by green welting update a traditional dining table, as does the disco-ball-like iron and mirrored light fixture. A patterned Beauvais carpet in brown, aubergine, and cream breaks up the solids.

Katie's teal sideboard, featuring leather panels and overscale Du Verre "Pomegranate" hardware in a bronze finish, holds its own against glossy, Granny Smith–apple green walls.

setting them off against silver-papered walls.

For Katie, just as a matching suite of furniture kills the appearance of a dining room, hard chairs ruin a dinner party. Softness is all too often missing from a dining room, not only visually but in terms of comfort. Katie's answer? Full curtains, an unusual rug, preferably antique, and upholstered chairs. A solid, cushioned back and seat allow guests to settle in for a relaxed meal and afford Katie another opportunity to introduce color and texture. She often uses different fabrics on the front and back of the chair, usually a solid toward the table and a pattern facing out, thereby giving the central grouping of furniture its own lively façade.

To Katie an intimate table, seating no more than eight, works best. It allows for lively conversation without the swiveling from side to side that larger tables impose on dinner companions. (Because the empty horizontal surface of larger tables can make a dining room look lonely, Katie often dresses them with objects beyond table settings.) A table for eight also makes finding a set of chairs easier or having a set made more affordable. For

The Ideal Dining Chair

Trial and error have produced a formula that Katie turns to again and again.

- ◆ **Form:** an armless upholstered chair with wooden legs
- ◆ **Width:** 20" (the optimum balance between a commodious seat and fitting chairs around a table)
- ◆ **Seat height:** 18½" maximum
- ◆ **Chair back height:** 36" to 43" maximum
- ◆ **Chair back pitch:** 3.5"
- ◆ **Seat material:** solid-colored ultrasuede or mohair, both hard wearing and easy to maintain
- ◆ **Exterior back material:** anything at all, as long as it's an interesting partner to the seat material, usually a decorative pattern to offset the solid color of the seat
- ◆ **Trim:** nailheads, contrast piping
- ◆ **Final detail:** felt disks on the underside of the feet

bigger gatherings, Katie usually provides for another table and has a seamstress make up matching tablecloths. Folding chairs (Katie likes bamboo) or side chairs retrieved from elsewhere in the house provide extra seating.

Because of its nocturnal habits, a dining room needs special attention when it comes to lighting. Not only does Katie make a point of installing unusual chandeliers—everything from mirrored globes to Murano glass antiques to exotic lanterns—but she also adds other light sources like sconces and tries to incorporate something reflective in every dining room. Mirror, crystal, art under glass, and glossy paint all contribute extra sparkle by bouncing light around. Silver leaf and polished metal like brass and silver provide softer luster. Silk shades on lamps and wall sconces echo the glow of candlelight. Believing that you can't have too many various light sources, as long as they are all equipped with dimmers, Katie will even install downlights in the ceiling, usually pindot size. Plenty of lighting has the added advantage of allowing you to go darker and more daring with wall color.

Antique Swedish bird prints positioned around a pair of Italian sconces from the 1950s temper the field of bright green. A pair of ceramic swan tureens extends the bird theme.

OPPOSITE The dining room of an oceanfront house references the sea, in warm tones. Butternut squash–colored wallpaper in an Art Nouveau pattern envelops the room while chairs painted an orangy red echo the faux coral of the chandelier.

ABOVE Katie's sideboard of pearwood and shagreen fills a niche and supports a pair of Murano lamps that, like the chandelier and the painting, add bright notes of red to a color scheme of cool blues and greens. A sheer embroidered panel behind silk curtains disguises an uninspiring view.

Katie found a single eighteenth-century Italian chair in the attic of this Virginia house and had eleven more made for its grand dining room. An antique Indian mirror hangs on walls lined in blond horsehair, an expensive but appropriate material for this house in horse country. Grasscloth, a Katie favorite, produces a similar warm-textured effect at a far more modest cost.

A deep and soft gray-brown coats both walls and trim in a dining room meant not just for dining. Katie finds that deep colors lend a sophisticated mood and glamour to dining rooms. Figurative grass-cloth on the ceiling references the palette of the antique Persian carpet. Coral-colored silk embroidered with a brown geometric pattern wraps the back of chairs with mohair seats.

Furnishing a dining room with more than a table and chairs makes it much more inviting, and more useful. The sofa was designed to fit in a niche between a bookcase and a doorway. Its seat is at dining height so that it can also be used as a banquette when the dining table is placed in front of it. Picture lights and sconces with silk shades add just the right amount of glow to dark walls.

ABOVE Curtains in teal wool sateen reference the elegant two-tone green boiserie of this New York dining room while adding a bolder note. The carpet inspired the motif for the pelmet's embroidered felt embellishments.

OPPOSITE Silver sets this dining room aglitter. Above sari-like curtains of metallic fabric, ceiling panels lined in silver wallpaper glow. Silver leaf frames the mirror and giant cabbage roses stenciled in silver on deep blue walls wrap the room.

ABOVE LEFT The quiet palette of an outdoor dining area composed of warm wood furniture and cushions in soft blue suits the view of natural marshes extending to the sea.

ABOVE RIGHT The petals of fresh flowers replicate the pattern on the surface of an antique ceramic vase.

LEFT Settees and low tables form an inviting, cozy corner near an outdoor fireplace on Nantucket that's perfect for breakfast, an informal lunch, or cocktails in the evening.

OPPOSITE The deep finish of a steel dining table and pierced lanterns echo the dark painted trim of a covered terrace, a handsome complement to the light warm stone.

LEFT Katie added iridescent trim to orange silk curtains and silver leaf to the ceiling to lend her own dining room a quality she strives for in rooms used mostly at night: luminosity. The lacy form of a bamboo chair from Hong Kong is highlighted by its placement in front of French doors.

OPPOSITE Appliquéd evil eyes of red Thai silk embellish custom dining chairs upholstered in yellow silk and gray mohair, a combining of contrasting fabrics that is a Katie signature. A vintage fixture of carved glass beads adds a glow at night, while grasscloth walls and a sisal carpet soften hard surfaces.

OPPOSITE The shape of an antique Venetian mirror echoes the configuration of a New York dining room. Notes of blue and red—printed silk curtains, an antique Iznik bowl, a watercolor by David Ambrose, a branch of coral—enliven muted walls of camel-colored ultrasuede and chairs in bronze textured cotton.

ABOVE Silver wallpaper cut into squares masquerades as silver leaf in a California dining room. The sunbursts dotting the walls are resin tiebacks painted the same deep Chinese red as the woodwork. A collection of blue-and-white ginger jars is a traditional yet unexpected complement to Chippendale dining chairs.

ABOVE Gilded dining chairs pick up the gold thread seen in fretwork molding, a Chinoiserie bench, and an antique screen in a hall off the dining room.

OPPOSITE Dining room walls in a lighter and greener blue than the cobalt of the living room beyond are a lively backdrop to the traditional mahogany dining table and chairs. Peacock blue welting outlines cushions of pale green-yellow mohair made for the chairs.

LEFT An American milk-glass chandelier, faux-bois chairs painted pale lavender, grasscloth walls, and a bare wood floor set a more informal tone for a dining room in a house near the beach. Dining rooms are perfect places to display collections, especially of fragile objects.

ABOVE A cupboard accented with faux malachite, one of a pair, originally belonged to Jacqueline Onassis. The original bright lavender interior suggested the addition of other purples to a room showcasing a collection of blue-and-white ceramics.

ABOVE Proving that more is sometimes best, Katie added, to great effect, a hand-loomed wool carpet in a Moorish motif to a dining room already singing with pattern from a custom Fromental wallpaper.

OPPOSITE Tendrils of cherry blossoms in unexpected yellows and oranges practically disappear into the ikat pattern of the dining chair fabric. The wavy front of a 1930s mirrored cabinet has a funhouse effect on the carpet.

Kitchens

*"For most clients, the kitchen is the center of the house.
It has to do it all. But why miss out on the wow factor?"*

EW ROOMS HAVE AS MUCH going on in them as the kitchen. Aside from being the place where food is prepared, it's where family gathers, close friends are entertained, homework is done, the calendar is kept, flowers are arranged. It's usually everyone's favorite room in the house and definitely the site of the most comings and goings. No other room has to serve as many functions or constituents, and for that reason, Katie likes to keep it simple.

As with bathrooms, a white kitchen provides a clean, bright environment in which to take care of business. It's Katie's favorite color for kitchens, but those she designs are far from bland or monochromatic because, like an intuitive cook, she adds the right ingredients in order to bring to the table an enticing, well-balanced creation. Her kitchens are efficient for the cook, hospitable for guests, user-friendly to families, altogether inviting yet entirely sophisticated. There is always something you want to borrow from a Katie Ridder kitchen.

Because cupboards constitute the main architectural element of the kitchen, that's where Katie focuses her attention first. More important than precisely what style of cabinetry—though her preference is for a plain panel door—is its proportion and arrangement. She groups and stacks cabinets, often running them nearly the full height of a wall, so that there is a good balance of open wall space to storage. If the cupboards stop short of the ceiling, she paints the remaining strip of wall the same color as the wood of the cabinets so nothing interrupts the eye. Kitchenware that is

A bright, comfortable eating area eclectically furnished with a banquette and chairs around a pedestal table is a hallmark of Katie's kitchens. In a sunny kitchen in Connecticut, the boldly colored Josef Frank fabric of the roman shade ties together a banquette upholstered in crimson shagreenlike leather and a beaded chandelier by Marjorie Skouras. Chairs in natural rush and oak balance a metallic table base topped by cool terrazzo.

In this Nantucket kitchen, glass globes caught in wire netting evoke
nautical floats and the blue herringbone tile backsplash suggests the sea.

needed infrequently, like holiday bakeware or large tabletop pieces for entertaining, can go in the highest cupboards.

Lower cabinets are a combination of drawers and doors, and a pullout trash bin with two compartments. Countertops are usually honed Carrara marble, a quartz-like composite material, or stainless steel, all of which reflect light. As do backsplashes of painted glass and whole walls of glazed tile, low-maintenance materials Katie uses to spice the kitchen with color. For upper cabinets, she often turns to glass-fronted doors to break up the expanse of an otherwise solid plane at eye level. Ribbed glass has the effect of a slightly out-of-focus photograph. You see everything, just not so clearly, which not only adds a little mystery but is more forgiving of less-than-compulsive housekeepers. For food storage, space permitting, Katie builds in a pantry. The open shelves make finding things easy yet the cacophony of packaging is tucked behind a door.

Quantity of space determines much of how a kitchen is configured. When there is room for an island, Katie includes one but positions it so that it maintains the efficiency of a cook-friendly galley layout with the stove and sink arranged opposite each other. For in-kitchen dining, a combination of chair and banquette seating around a table is her favorite. To ease access for diners, the table almost always has a pedestal base, usually a metal one she orders from a restaurant supply house, topped by a custom top in a terrazzo-like composite material. Banquettes save floor space, can squeeze in more diners, and are kid-friendly, informal, and fun. They're also a great device for introducing a big block of color into the kitchen.

Beyond square footage, light is the other factor that drives Katie's arrangement of a kitchen. Whenever possible, she suggests positioning the sink in front of or near a window. Aside from providing the room's primary workstation with the best illumination of all—daylight—it affords the cook or clean-up crew a view. Kitchen windows are shaded preferably with nothing at all, but when privacy's an issue, Katie installs either wooden blinds or solar shades. When the sun goes down, Katie lights up the kitchen with a combination of multiple recessed or surface-mounted lights spaced evenly across the ceiling, under-cabinet lighting, and a pendant fixture or two to create a more intimate space over a counter or table.

Katie's Favorite Materials and Furnishings for a Hard-working *and* Stylish Kitchen

- **Countertops:** Carrara marble or a manufactured look-alike such as Silestone in a light color
- **Hardware:** stainless-steel handles from Sugatsune
- **Lighting:** modern pendant fixtures from Artemide, Flos, Design Within Reach
- **Floor:** wood or cork
- **Tile:** from Ann Sacks, Mosaic House
- **Banquette fabric:** synthetic "glazed linen" look-alike or leather
- **Chair:** classic bistro chairs in 20 different colors and 24 weave patterns by Maison Gatti from Style by Annick de Lorme
- **Table:** pedestal base with terrazzo-like composite top from Durite Concepts

OPPOSITE The door of a flower-cutting room in Arkansas is, aptly, a greener hue than the pale powder of the kitchen it adjoins. Ebonized wood floors flow throughout.

RIGHT Upper cabinets, accessible by a rolling library ladder, reach all the way to the kitchen's high ceiling. All hardware is nickel-plated, including the ladder's rail.

ABOVE A banquette of embossed leather accented with nailheads turns a bay window into a comfortable place to relax as well as dine. Wood blinds, a wood tabletop, and a paisley shade for the hanging fixture also contribute to creating a warm entertaining area of the kitchen.

OPPOSITE Ribbed-glass cabinet panels, glass-composite counters, stainless steel, and ebonized floors ensure that natural light penetrates deep into a spacious kitchen in Arkansas. Katie prefers the clean approach of unadorned windows near food-prep areas. The distinctly shapely silhouette of Cherner stools tempers the mass of the central island.

ABOVE AND RIGHT A Delft tile backsplash, an antique brass billiard light, and a nineteenth-century marble-topped pedestal table suit the elegance of a beautifully proportioned Virginia kitchen.

ABOVE Moroccan mosaic tile extends the silver tones of stainless-steel appliances and a custom steel-and-glass stove hood. A predominantly white kitchen is a clean fresh place to cook, but it shouldn't feel clinical; Katie always tosses in some color to humanize the space.

OPPOSITE Alternating stripes of quartersawn white oak and thermo-treated oak put a bold floor underfoot in an otherwise monochromatic kitchen. Blue lights overhead bring a touch of sky inside.

A framed Arts and Crafts textile adds a welcome "window" of blue to a New York kitchen. French encaustic floor tiles and a banquette modeled after one in London contribute Old World notes. A grid of half-mirrored bulbs screwed into custom "peony" metal fixtures designed by Katie gives far more even, and useful, light than a single overhead fixture.

LEFT A panel of printed velvet set into a banquette of purple glazed synthetic raffia adds a touch of elegance to an eating area furnished with modern white chairs and light fixtures.

OPPOSITE Katie frequently specs French bistro chairs in custom colors, here white and cherry to pick up the red of the leather banquette, of a stripe in the sheer window panel, and in a creamsicle print by Donald Baechler.

A Moorish-style screen of laser-cut Corian opens the kitchen to an adjacent playroom/sitting room. The red banquette of a wipable glazed linenlike fabric echoes the red in a playful Calder print.

Back-painted glass makes a seamless backsplash that's easy to maintain and subtly reflective. Here, the French blue balances the red of the kitchen's eating area (opposite).

Cherry cabinetry reminiscent of turn-of-the-twentieth-century butler's pantries suits the kitchen of a traditional house in San Francisco. Walls lined in Mediterranean tiles featuring a leafy medallion and a plaid banquette beneath a deep-set ogee window flesh out the historic character.

An oversize hood of steel and glass helps to anchor a large central island in a kitchen composed of planes of light, reflective materials like ribbed glass, and stainless steel.

Using tile wall-to-wall instead of limiting it to a backsplash is a favorite Katie technique. Moroccan tiles made up of smaller glazed zellige tiles in blue-green, gray, and soft white "paper" the walls of a Pebble Beach, California, kitchen with an unobstructed view of the golf course and the ocean. Logico Mini Triple Nested ceiling fixtures float like clouds above an antique rug and an African stool.

A window frame painted apple green picks up the wall color of a back hall and of the green in Katie's "Seaweed" wallpaper, which lines the mudroom. Vintage Murano glass hankerchief shades appear to ride the fresh breezes wafting through this oceanfront house.

OPPOSITE A collection of framed botanical specimens found in the Paris flea market serves as a frieze for a sunny green-yellow Northern California kitchen.

ABOVE Blond wood chairs with woven wood backs extend the natural palette of the maple butcher-block counter and tabletop, a tonal match for the aged paper of the framed botanicals.

Bedrooms

"Leaving a box spring exposed is like leaving the house without your shoes—a situation that's undressed, and easily corrected."

No other room is as dominated by a single piece of furniture as the bedroom. And no piece of furniture is more unwieldy than a bed. Its expanse is a wide visual plateau that all designers wrestle with. Armed with a strong sense of scale and aided by her love of textiles, Katie relishes turning a design liability into an asset. By celebrating the bed rather than downplaying it with a monotone palette or disguising it with a cascade of pillows, she transforms her bedrooms into places as appealing to be in by day as to sleep in at night.

Upholstered headboards in a great variety of profiles and fabrics are one of Katie's favorite ways to highlight the bed and a signature of her bedrooms. Like a crown, they set off the head of the bed, lifting the eye. They also anchor the bed in the room by outlining its place. Functionally, nothing is more practical. A cushioned headboard is comfortable to lean against, takes up little space, and provides a great canvas for color and texture. When Katie does use bed frames, almost always of wood or metal, they tend to be either antique, a sentimental favorite of a client, or a practical solution (bunk beds, daybeds with trundles) for kids' rooms that need to accommodate sleepovers and evolving taste.

Beyond distinctive headboards and bedsteads, Katie often turns to bed hangings to lend a bedroom more warmth, color, and "architecture." Canopy beds, especially four-posters with curtains, create an intimate room within a room and work particularly well in large bedrooms, where the bed can seem adrift in an ocean of space. Even in smaller bedrooms, though, Katie will use fabric to create a nook, tucking a bed into an alcove of fabric as simple as a pelmet with curtain panels. In a room where so much surface

An Indian curtain fabric inspired the motif for the Turkish carnations embroidered on a headboard produced by Lisa Fine. Grosgrain ribbon bordering the lampshade is a deeper version of the lavender wall color. If there is one standout hallmark of a bedroom by Katie, it is a well-detailed headboard in an unusual shape.

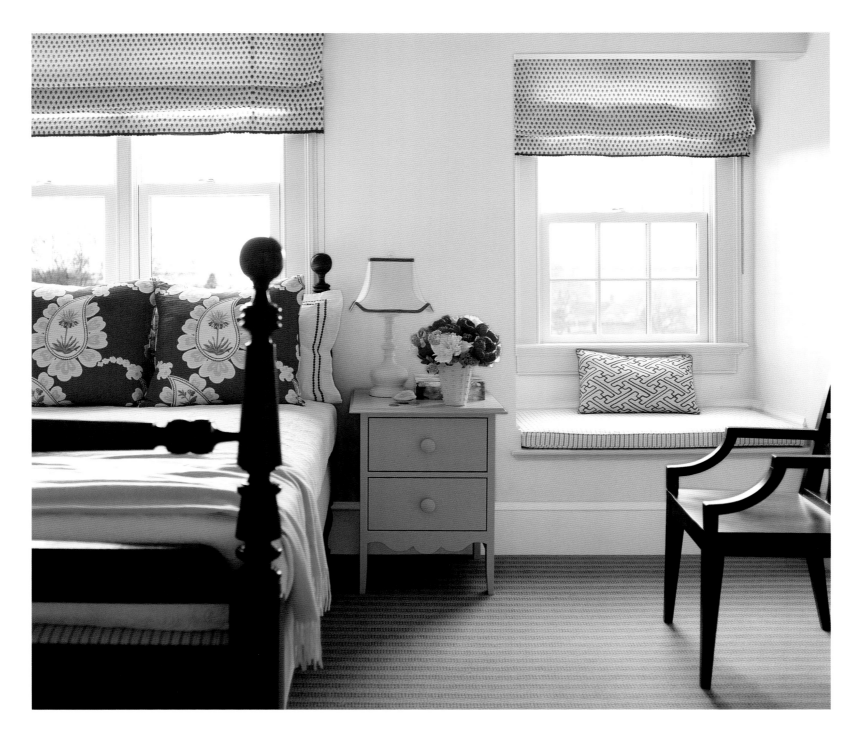

A palette of raspberry-accented textiles and apple green walls brightens a third-floor bedroom with a view of the Rhode Island coast. The antique cannonball bed was placed against the windows to save space. Like most of Katie's rooms for children, this one for a young girl is bright but not juvenile.

s horizontal, curtains are a vertical element that provides visual balance.

Whether the bedroom is expansive or cozy, Katie finds a solution that makes it inviting and personalizes it. For the master bedroom in a grand historic house, she installed a stately bed composed of an elaborate footboard made to mimic an antique headboard, a pelmet fashioned from an antique tapestry, and elegant bed curtains. For a more modest bedroom tucked under the roof of a house by the sea, she placed a family heirloom bedstead right up against a pair of windows and loaded the room with lively color. In a narrow city bedroom, she positioned the long side of a single bed against the wall and made it a lounge-y destination by adding bolsters, decorative pillows, and an unusual half tester above.

The size of a bedroom is not nearly as important to Katie as certain comforts that should never be compromised, starting with a good bed. Those handmade by Beckley, consisting of upholstered box spring, headboard, and horsehair mattress, are her favorites. Though expensive, they compare favorably to buying a quality mattress and box spring, and then having a seamstress make a custom bedskirt and an upholsterer a separate headboard. Given its role as the host of the room, it's important for a bed to be attired in a "suit" that's both tailored and stylish.

Since the bedroom is used more at night than any other room, thoughtful lighting from multiple sources is essential. Like many designers, Katie would happily dispense with overhead fixtures in a bedroom for the unflattering light they cast. But, ever practical, she acknowledges their usefulness as another light source that can quickly illuminate a space, so she tracks down pendant lights interesting enough to justify their presence. Otherwise, lighting is a combination of bedside table lamps, reading lights, and floor lamps that cast light at more or less the same level. Multiple pools of warm, welcoming light is the goal.

Katie's ideal checklist of furniture in a bedroom includes: a bed with an upholstered or covered box spring, bedside tables with open and closed storage, a comfortable reading chair, with an ottoman if space permits, a desk and side chair, and a dresser when closet storage is not sufficient. If she had her way, televisions would be excluded, but far more clients want them than don't, so she accommodates them by installing a bookcase or étagère opposite the bed that incorporates a TV without accentuating it. Tying all the furnishings together is carpet that runs wall-to-wall, or nearly so in cases where exposing some floor is preferable, for maximum comfort and sound insulation. Window treatments are usually floor-length curtains or Roman shades, sometimes a combination of the two.

Beyond all the components and functional considerations, a bedroom should feel like a sanctuary, consistently comfortable and pleasurably restful. That doesn't mean it need slip into design somnolence. Just as much as a public room, it ought to surprise and stimulate, something that form, color, texture, and unexpected touches can accomplish.

How to Dress a Bed, Katie-style

- Use ivory cotton sheets with decoration limited to an embroidered band on the top sheet
- Turn the top sheet down over a cotton piqué blanket, neatly tucked in at the bottom and sides
- Arrrange three different sizes of pillows, from back to front:
  - Two king shams
  - Two standard-size pillows
  - One small decorative pillow like a boudoir or lumbar pillow to break up the expanse
- Place a down duvet (covered in lightweight decorative sheeting material) at the foot of the bed, folded in thirds so that it is easy to pull up

ABOVE Florals from Provençal to Chinese and a palette embracing warm and cool colors produce a richly textured yet soothing bedroom. The headboard features a mitered border composed of embroidered strips removed from a length of the blue fabric. Beds offer an opportunity to play with textiles, and Katie takes full advantage of it.

OPPOSITE Layers of pattern—gingko-embroidered sheets, an Arts and Crafts–style bedspread, a crewelwork pillow—dress a reproduction Raj bed flanked by red leather tables and cloisonné lamps. Nightstands with both a drawer and open shelving are a Katie favorite.

OPPOSITE A boy's room in a New York apartment facing the East River aptly catches waves in its headboard and box spring, as well as in stenciled whitecaps inspired by a motif by Arts and Crafts architect and designer C.F.A. Voysey. The table with climbing animals is an antique.

ABOVE In a wide bay window, an antique sofa upholstered in a cotton stripe hides a radiator and allows room for curtains to fall to either side.

ABOVE Block-printed curtains, an antique octagonal bedside table, sunburst mirrors, and an embroidered headboard strike a decorative yet casual balance for a bedroom in a Hamptons house.

OPPOSITE To make the most of tight dimensions, Katie centered her younger daughter's bed in the gable end of the room, incorporating window curtains into a canopy that frames a headboard produced by Lisa Fine. Cocoa-colored walls—a departure for a young girl's room—are brightened by pinks and apple green.

Headboards, four ways

ABOVE LEFT A Thai lamp picks up the red cotton welting outlining the Indian profile of a headboard upholstered in tobacco-colored corduroy.

ABOVE RIGHT Celery walls set off a range of purples, from the deep violet of the linen headboard to Euro pillows in a heathered-lavender linen trimmed in olive moss fringe to lighter lavender boudoir pillows to neckroll pillows in palest purple.

LEFT Nailheads accentuate the ziggurat profile of a headboard that contrasts with the curves of a painted desk, a gourd-like lamp, and a klismos chair.

OPPOSITE No detail is overlooked in a bedroom featuring a custom-quilted cotton headboard, a silk shade trimmed with black metallic thread, a nailhead-accented faux-sharkskin table, and bed linens embroidered with a continuous gold loop.

OPPOSITE In a Hamptons bedroom with a beadboard tray ceiling, an iron canopy shapes an intimate space for the bed. A striped Beauvais carpet picks up the lines of the beadboard, while curtains in a Scalamandré silk ikat add a bolder abstract pattern.

ABOVE An iron canopy forms a simple frame for an elaborate headboard of metallic embroidery on cotton and silk. Sheer bed curtains extend the delicate air of the walls, which are lined in silk embroidered with leaves.

ABOVE In a San Francisco bedroom, the multiple cubbyholes of a dramatically painted eighteenth-century Italian secretary display a collection of silver horse trophy cups.

RIGHT An antique tapestry, pressed into service as a valance, inspired the embroidered borders of linen curtain panels for an elaborate canopy bed. A horsehair chest opposite a pair of club chairs in cut velvet conceals a TV.

ABOVE A fanciful pelmet, its profile derived from a window pattern in a royal Indian residence, lends the daybed in a teenager's room the air of a divan in a Mughal palace. A windowlike antique mirror, a hanging fixture of pierced brass, and toss pillows in assorted patterns contribute to the lounge-y atmosphere.

OPPOSITE A custom bed upholstered in red cotton tucks into a nook formed by curtains and a shallow pelmet of embroidered silk. The fabric shades of swinging sconces pick up the cheerful pattern of the toss pillow, while red embroidered stripes on the sheets echo the piping of the tiebacks and pelmet.

OPPOSITE Terra-cotta banding highlights the architectural eccentricities of Katie's bedroom. A Swedish fabric featuring buckeye leaves brings the treetops inside, while more stylized leaves with trapunto veins form the back of a daybed.

ABOVE A children's book with lots of curlicues inspired the profile for the headboard of Katie's silk velvet Beckley bed. A Curtis Jere metal sculpture floats above a fireplace "mantel" that is nothing more than a bolection molding painted green. A sea fan in soft pink crowns the bed.

OPPOSITE In a quiet corner of Katie's bedroom, tall bronze candlestick lamps topped by pale blue silk shades mirror the twin pedestals of a desk, and matching chair, in the Biedermeier style.

ABOVE In an anteroom to the bedroom, Katie's "Attendants" wallpaper adds exotic flavor to a Regency-style oeil-de-boeuf window of amber, blue, green, and clear glass.

ABOVE A radiant pillow fashioned from an antique obi and a Spitzmiller lamp with a gold glaze complement a turn-of-the-twentieth-century suite of japanned furniture in a Japanese pavilion on an American estate.

OPPOSITE Cotton banding marking the seams of tatami mats references the wood structure framing restored murals. Contemporary garden stools in bright yellow cozy up to Victorian wicker chairs painted black.

LEFT Beneath the painted tray ceiling of a guesthouse bedroom on Nantucket, a Raoul cotton printed with old-fashioned flowers lines the walls, curtains the windows, and even wraps closet fronts. Against the surround of pattern, a custom blue bed dressed in crisp white sheets is cool and inviting.

OPPOSITE An antique quilted textile covers the top of a John Roselli bed that features a rope base in a basketweave pattern. Warm "paper bag" brown walls complement American antiques like the whale, stork, and chest of drawers. A pale, textured carpet balances darker walls and makes for a soft landing.

OPPOSITE Swedish country beds with padded insets of fern-printed linen flank a table lacquered bright green in a guestroom painted a yellow-green as refreshing as limeade. The box springs are upholstered in a delicate stripe.

ABOVE Matching maple double beds copied from American antiques and dressed in summery blue-and-white-striped blankets fill the eaves of a room papered in an old-fashioned all-over print.

ABOVE In a Connecticut bedroom, a glazed-ceramic drum table reflects a silk dhurrie with a Moorish motif. A pillow in Katie's "Attendants" pattern dresses up a Lawson sofa in blue mohair next to a plaster floor lamp modeled on a design by Dorothy Draper.

RIGHT Circles on a pair of vintage ceramic lamps from Daniel Barney extend the sunburst motif embroidered on the headboard in a Nantucket guestroom. The iridescent, pleated-silk trim of the blue wool sateen curtains is as fresh as a just-clipped grassy border.

OPPOSITE An Arkansas bedroom features striking walls of green silk with peacock blue trim, one of Katie's favorite color combinations. A fire blazes in a blue glazed-tile hearth, with a reproduction octagonal mirror and a mirrored dance hall fixture from the 1950s adding further sparkle.

ABOVE Cranberry grosgrain ribbon trims roman shades of Muriel Brandolini fabric above a bench upholstered in an ikat from Madeline Weinrib.

In a girl's bedroom in Arkansas, a carpet with an all-over Greek key pattern from Stark playfully spars with Beckley beds covered in an Allegra Hicks printed cotton. Deep pink pompoms outline the seams of custom shades for a vintage lamp.

LEFT A vintage map of America, its mat the same navy blue as that of the daybed, provides educational art for a boy's bedroom. At the window, Josef Frank's "Terrazzo" fabric reads like abstract planets lost in space.

OPPOSITE Built-in open and closed storage provides organized display space and forms an alcove for an upholstered daybed in a boy's room. Pillows with an oversize monogram, Josef Frank's "Manhattan" printed cotton at the window and covering a bedside sconce, and a pair of green, stacking child's chairs spell fun.

OPPOSITE A ceiling covered in green-on-silver Mylar wallpaper adds shimmer to a room for a girl who loves turquoise. Custom embroidered linens reinterpret the sprightly pattern of the Cowtan & Tout cotton covering the daybed.

ABOVE In a Rhode Island summer house, twin boys share a room outfitted with hard-wearing furnishings like a sturdy Pottery Barn bunk bed, moving-pad-like blankets, and sconces that could have come from a ship's chandlery. Katie's own "Beetlecat" wallpaper captures sailboats coming and going.

ABOVE Blues and golden browns captured in a Swedish printed cotton dress Katie's son's bed. Modern notes like a bentwood bedside table, Lucite shelves holding colorful model cars, and a leather-clad bench by Katie balance traditional brass sconces and a collection of European garden prints.

RIGHT The centerpiece of Katie's older daughter's bedroom is a melon linen headboard based on the profile of the Chippendale mirror on the wall and embellished with her embroidered monogram. Brass and porcelain Chinese lamps pick up the deep orange of Katie's "Leaf" wallpaper.

OPPOSITE In a girl's room painted uncharacteristically brown, printed linen curtains form a canopy around a raspberry-colored headboard with an Italian profile. A Capiz shell chandelier and a custom quilt sprinkle additional sophisticated pattern high and low.

ABOVE A pale blue club chair outlined in pink and accented with a Judy Ross hand-embroidered pillow is joined by a leather pouf and a ceramic stool. The birds-on-branches floor lamp demonstrates that children's furnishings can be whimsical without being juvenile.

Bathrooms

"Powder rooms, because they are stand-alone spaces hidden behind a door, are places to be a little extravagant, with decoration or materials or both. Ensuite bathrooms I design in tandem with the bedroom."

FIRST AND FOREMOST, A BATH- room needs to have a fresh, sparkling air, and nothing spells clean like shiny white porcelain. Katie loves a white bathroom or, more specifically, white bathroom fixtures—sink, tub, toilet. Yet, like any other room she decorates, Katie's bathrooms blossom with color. Clean is one thing; clinical is another. Just because a bathroom is a utilitarian space doesn't mean you can't have a little fun. Color brings life to a room you spend a considerable amount of time in. Plus, nothing sets off white fixtures like a contrasting hue.

In her bathrooms, Katie tends to strike a balance between white and color in one of two ways. When the floor and ceiling are white, then color goes on the walls, either as tile—again in a hue with presence—or as wallpaper in unusual colors and patterns. Heavily trafficked bathrooms may get a wear-and-tear-resistant dado of tile or beadboard, with only the higher section of wall covered in wallpaper. And if the room presents some odd angle or otherwise awkward architecture, she might run the wallpaper right up to and over the ceiling. Not only can wallpaper make a bathroom (a space often neglected in terms of decoration) feel complete, it can hide a host of sins.

In bathrooms where the walls and ceiling are white or light, then color goes on the floor, usually in the form of tile in a strong shade or a bold pattern. Large tiles from Morocco bring the two together seamlessly. One of Katie's favorite and signature materials, these encaustic cement tiles come in patterns from classical to exotic to whimsical. Smooth to the feet yet not slippery, they're cool in summer and can be soothingly warm in winter if

Like a spring garden in full bloom, the grassy green walls of a powder room in San Francisco are strewn with hand-painted tin flowers modeled after botanically correct antique versions in porcelain. A nineteenth-century rococo mirror framed in cobalt glass and gilt wood reflects a window to a courtyard. Katie often turns to antique or unusual mirrors to dress up powder rooms and bathrooms.

radiant heat is installed. Because Moroccan tiles are not widely used in this country, they create a lively and unusual "carpet" seldom seen in a bathroom.

Rarely is one of Katie's bathrooms without an element of surprise, especially when she takes on the decoration of powder rooms. Because no one lingers in them for long, powder rooms can support far more drama than regular bathrooms. And because they're typically quite small rooms, just large enough to accommodate a sink and toilet, they provide perfect opportunities to use more expensive materials economically. This is the place to install sconces, a chandelier, or a mirror not typically designated for a bathroom. Or to use an antique chest or table as the base for a sink. Or to hang art, as moisture is rarely an issue.

Katie goes as wild in the powder room as clients will allow. She has stenciled walls with branches, leaves, and flowers. She has covered walls with panels of *verre églomisé*. She transformed one powder room into an aquarium by encircling the space with wallpaper printed with schools of carp and another into a fantasy garden by mounting three-dimensional blossoms on walls lacquered a grassy green. For the latter, Katie found an artist to reproduce in tin, then hand-paint, 150 botanically correct flowers inspired by porcelain models made in the Sèvres workshop. The effect of

Katie's Dream Bathroom

- Radiant heated floor
- One's own sink
- A bathtub big enough for soaking, with a handheld shower attachment
- Even light
- Lots of counter space
- Lots of storage
- Moroccan-tiled walls and/or floors
- A combination of towel bars and hooks
- A plug inside a cabinet for a blow dryer

this "powder room as jewel box," as Katie calls it, was so striking that Ozzie Osborne borrowed the design for a hallway in his house.

Even a regular bathroom can have moments of high style and unexpected decoration. Lighting and mirrors are great vehicles for delivering a special aura to a functional space. A sparkly chandelier provides something to focus on while in the tub, prompting flights of fancy. Nautical lights are fitting bathroom sconces in a seaside house. If space permits, a lamp on a table lends a bathroom a softer, more furnished feel, as do silk shades on wall sconces.

Though Katie's clients often ask for medicine cabinets, she's more inclined to build in handy storage near the sink, freeing up a mirror to be any size and framed in almost any material, from gilded wood to cobalt glass to woven rush. As a material, mirror is affordable, easy to maintain, and simpler to install than tile. Nothing's more effective at enlarging a small space or bouncing light around. A mirror that runs wall to wall, or nearly, above a sink (or two) can visually double the size of a room, just as sconces mounted directly on the mirror give the impression of double the light. With any bathroom, the goal is a clean, well-lighted space. Katie's bathrooms have the extra dash that makes them rooms you want to spend time in.

Oversize matte ivory subway tiles and a worker's-style sink lend a stylish yet utilitarian air to a third-floor kids' bathroom in a Rhode Island summer house. The woven frame of the mirror suits the casual environment. A printed-canvas tub that picks up the honeycomb of the hexagonal floor tiles holds towels edged in colorful cotton tape.

ABOVE The cobalt blue glass frame of an antique mirror matches the deep blue of flowers scattered across a whimsical wallpaper depicting birds dangling pocket watches and other items from their beaks. A wood chest of drawers warms the palette.

OPPOSITE Iridescent silver carp on a de Gournay wallpaper circle a powder room where the bubbly glass of vintage Italian sconces and Lalique-like frosted-glass tap handles extend the watery theme.

LEFT In a bathroom tight on space, a bin for towels is built in under the sink and a single chrome light fixture is mounted over the mirror. Josef Frank wallpaper is a colorful counterpoint to otherwise white surfaces.

OPPOSITE The emerald green palette of a bathroom is an extension of the adjacent bedroom with curtains in a green-and-blue cotton stripe from Lulu DK. A looped mirror picks up the black lines of the fishing-net design of a vintage wallpaper from Secondhand Rose.

ABOVE LEFT An elegant, burnished-metal tub from Waterworks occupies its own windowed bay in a bathroom in Arkansas. Peacock blue trim picks up the deepest color in Katie's Turkish-inspired "Attendants" wallpaper.

ABOVE RIGHT A vanity on one side, twin sinks on the other, and mirrors above create an infinity effect. A band of polished nickel ringing the room extends the shimmer of the mirrors. A touch of red on the sconces spices the cool palette of the room.

OPPOSITE An antique stool with a practical terry-cloth-covered seat tucks under a Carrara marble vanity trimmed in polished nickel strips and handles to match the bathroom faucets. The wide mirror, with sconces installed atop it, visually doubles the space.

OPPOSITE The only thing as fresh as white in a bathroom is blue. With every inch of wall covered in variegated turquoise tiles from Ann Sacks, a California bathroom seems immersed in tropical waters. Against the watery tiles, the Candide tub from Waterworks takes on the aspect of a ship at sea.

ABOVE LEFT Blue cement tiles lining a tub alcove take on a livelier air as they wrap the sink in wainscoting, the tile profile forming a highly decorative border. The beaded ship fixture is vintage.

ABOVE RIGHT Glass tile in one-inch squares on the walls shifts to two-inch-square ceramic tile for the floor of a Park Avenue bathroom. The field of blue cleanly sets off white fixtures, including a custom vanity and a Silestone tub surround.

OPPOSITE Basketweave floor tile, extended to form a baseboard, picks up the warm wood of the vanity counter, as do faceted red glass knobs. Mirrors hung opposite each other produce an infinite vista.

ABOVE Natural materials like wood for countertops and a tub enclosure and wicker baskets for towels soften a Connecticut bathroom. The Asian motif on an area rug picks up the deep gray stone lining the shower.

LEFT Though the whale motif for an appliquéd privacy panel curtain by Penn & Fletcher came from a Swedish book, it references the heritage of this bathroom's location, Nantucket.

OPPOSITE In a Nantucket ground-floor bathroom with a great view, shutters mounted on only the lower half of the windows accommodate all degrees of privacy and openness. Terry cloth in a jaunty blue-and-white stripe covers a slipper chair.

Details

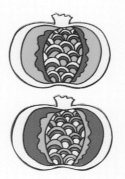

As much as color distinguishes Katie's work, it is the attention she lavishes on details that elevates her interiors to the level of couture. Like a designer adding the perfect fanciful flourish to a gown and insisting on hand-finished buttonholes, Katie focuses on details that reflect a fine hand and an artful eye, especially when applied to textiles. Her own love and appreciation of craft, color, and pattern turns up in signature upholstery treatments, lyrically graphic wallpapers of her own design, custom light fixtures accented with unusual trim or finials, and tilelike patterns in both contemporary carpets and walls of tile itself. Katie taps extraordinary sources for extravagant touches like the finest trapunto work, the best selection of antique textiles, and the most exquisite scenic wallpaper. But at the same time she herself will track down a ribbon in just the right hue to add to a lampshade, knowing full well the power of even a simple line of color to transform. With Katie's interiors, the thought that counts turns into the detail that shines.

Signature Katie touches—a brightly patterned woven carpet, furnishings in a mix of periods and styles, a colorful sofa incorporating an antique textile, and a custom shade of silk trimmed with velvet ribbon—transform the traditional dark study in her 1920s house into a welcoming hideout.

225

TOP ROW, LEFT TO RIGHT Red beads dot the edge of a hexagonal cotton shade mounted flush to the ceiling for a softer, more dimensional effect than a direct downlight. A long drum shade featuring Pierre Frey fabric is far spicier than your average kitchen light. Black ribbon ringing the tiers of a paper shade lends it a Wiener Werkstätte look.

BOTTOM ROW, LEFT TO RIGHT Hinged brass sconces with custom shades are Katie's favorite for bedside reading lights: cotton rickrack evokes American simplicity for a Nantucket bedroom; Katie's own bedside lamps feature green velvet ribbon a shade lighter than her olive-colored headboard and coral finials made by Eduardo Garza; delicate fringe is a subtle embellishment to sconces for a young girl's room.

Lighting

For Katie, lighting is just another exciting means of introducing shape, line, pattern, color, sparkle, natural elements, and atmosphere to a room. A firm believer that every room benefits from multiple sources of light, Katie takes full advantage of all the design opportunities that multiplicity affords. In a single room, she might deploy an antique chandelier, table lamps with bases made of a wide range of materials (ceramic, glass, japanned wood, resin, bronze, rush, sculpture), floor lamps, sconces, and picture lights. As much as she loves finding unusual fixtures, she is just as thrilled by, and adept at, creating her own.

For years Katie has worked closely with Susanne Wellott of Shades from the Midnight Sun, collaborating on everything from dramatic shades for entries to delicate shades for bedrooms. For a girl's room in a house at the shore, she fashioned a sprightly shade whose corners turn up in little kicks, all accented by raspberry-colored ribbon (see page 168). For cloisonné bedside lamps in a New York bedroom, bell-shaped shades feature silk in a swirling pattern edged by a narrow band of blue velvet ribbon (see page 171). Beyond satin, grosgrain, and velvet ribbon, Katie employs laser-cut ultrasuede, pompoms, beads, and even shells for extra-lively trim. Paper shades may sport a Provençal print or an Indian or Moorish motif. The soft light of silk, either plain or patterned and usually gathered, is a favorite for libraries and bedrooms.

For entries and hallways requiring more drama, Katie fashions shades resembling oversize Asian lanterns, made up in silk, often in red or orange hues, that lend a welcoming light and exotic air. Finally, like jewelry that finishes an outfit, finials by Katie are rarely standard issue and, in fact, often a custom ornament like metal enameled to resemble coral.

TOP A banded linen shade in a shape reminiscent of Turkish lanterns tops a candlestick desk lamp. A sprig of faux coral serves as the finial.

ABOVE Katie designed this hexagonal, celadon-trimmed lampshade using an Indian floral-motif fabric that echoes the celadon of the Ming vase.

DETAILS

Upholstery

W HEN IT COMES TO UPHOLSTERY, KATIE GOES WHERE few designers dare to tread, yet the liberties she takes with color, trim, and unusual textile pairings make her interiors sing. The forms she chooses for upholstered pieces are usually traditional; their covering, however, especially for chairs and ottomans, is anything but. At a minimum, contrast welting will highlight the lines of a club chair, and a pillow featuring an antique textile or an exotic pattern like an ikat will nestle in its contours. Dining chairs that feature altogether different fabrics front and back are a Katie signature. Often the seat and the seatback facing the table are a solid in an elegant tone, like a claret-colored mohair. In contrast, the back of the chair exposed to the rest of the room is, to Katie, a too-often-overlooked opportunity to enliven dining rooms with a refreshing dose of graphic pattern and rich color.

Recognizing that sofas are by nature substantial in size, presence, and investment, Katie most often treats them as a solid field of color meant to be accompanied by accents, either in the form of applied decoration or pillows in varied textiles. An unusual fabric like a Suzani may be integrated into the seatback of a sofa or an antique textile may form its skirt.

Katie's frequent collaborator in incorporating special fabrics and trims like obis and tapestry pieces into upholstered furniture and one-of-a-kind pillows is New York antique textile dealer Virginia Di Sciascio. Always, the goal is a balance of solid and pattern, accompanied by unexpected textures and colors.

CLOCKWISE FROM TOP LEFT S-shaped orange linen appliqués on a brown linen sofa. Green welting joins a woven cotton back and claret-colored mohair front on dining chairs. Deep pink welting draws a line along the edges of a club chair in a pale blue cut velvet. A panel of Uzbek embroidery is set into the seat cushion and back of a sofa in rose velvet. A Vanderhurd fabric covers the sides of a hexagonal ottoman with a glazed-calf top. Stylized flowers in wool crewelwork band the skirt of a linen sofa.

TOP ROW, LEFT TO RIGHT Katie removed an embroidered strip of a blue-and-white fabric to form a mitered border for a headboard. A stylized flower taken from a book on India embellishes, in stitching and appliqué, the seatback of a linen velvet dining chair. Katie's own dining chairs feature appliquéd evil eyes in red and white.

BOTTOM ROW, LEFT TO RIGHT An abstract pattern embroidered on a two-tone hexagonal ottoman squares off against a geometric wool carpet. A stitched espaliered vine fills the arched seatback of a green linen velvet dining chair finished with brass nailheads.

Embroidery

T HE NEEDLE ARTS HAVE BEEN A PASSION OF KATIE'S SINCE she was a ten-year-old making soft sculptures of birds and fish that she sold at shows in California. In her spare time, she still quilts, does needlepoint, and sews trim on pillows and curtains. As a decorator, she employs every embellishment in the book involving thread, yarn, fabric, and trim, from embroidery and trapunto to appliqué and crewelwork.

For her most elaborate designs, Katie turns to Penn & Fletcher, the legendary New York custom embroidery company led by Ernie Smith. Perhaps her most complex undertaking was a set of window treatments for a grand Italianate house in Virginia. Aside from commissioning the reproduction of elaborate gilded faux-bois valances based on an antique example, Smith designed a rich border of twigs, leaves, and berries for the pelmets and curtains that was expertly embroidered by Penn & Fletcher (see pages 70–71).

More commonly, the company embellishes sets of dining chairs for Katie, sometimes with a design confined to the backs of the chairs, sometimes with a motif that runs across both seat and back. A step up from using patterned fabric, custom embroidery on solid fabrics like silk and velvet turns chairs into one-of-a-kind heirlooms. Because any design can be executed, the embroidery can incorporate aspects of other furnishings or even more personal things like monograms. Katie's elder daughter's headboard features her initials in the form of a regal, oversize emblem (see pages 204–5).

TOP Silk cording in a linear geometric pattern that optically vibrates runs like a track up and over a pair of living room chairs upholstered in a yellowy green wool sateen by Holland & Sherry.

BOTTOM A silk headboard in the shape of a wide Moorish arch, delicately embroidered in India, is as exquisite as beautiful lingerie.

 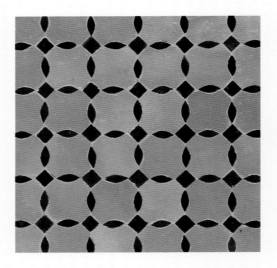 

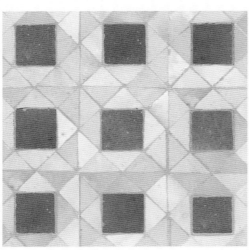  

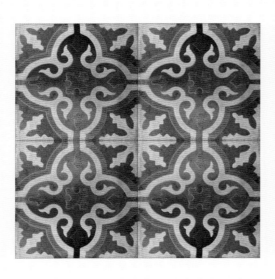  

TOP ROW, LEFT TO RIGHT
Midi zellige in red and white; Kora zellige in blue and black; Lucifer cement tile in gray, white, brown, and yellow.

MIDDLE ROW, LEFT TO RIGHT
Bassat in yellow and white; Rugosa cement tile in yellow, pale green, pink, brown, and red; Nejarine in light green and white.

BOTTOM ROW, LEFT TO RIGHT
Rosa cement tile in turquoise blue, gray, and white; Fleurs in pink and red; Metam in black, red, and white.

Tile

KATIE FIRST GREW ENAMORED OF THE DECORATIVE IMPACT OF handmade tile covering broad surfaces on visits to Turkey. But it is to Morocco that she most often turns for tile. Encaustic cement tiles with their multiplicity of colors and patterns can deliver looks from Old World to Victorian to mid-century geometric to utterly contemporary. With their completely flat, smooth, yet non-slippery surface, they are ideal flooring material for rooms subject to moisture like kitchens, bathrooms, and outdoor spaces. For Katie, the use of cement tiles in such places, where a real rug would not be suitable, is comparable to providing an interesting patterned carpet. Because kitchens need the quieting effect of solid-colored cabinetry that mates well with appliances, floor tile is a great means of introducing something lively yet not overwhelming. In Katie's kitchens, such tile has a comfortable yet sophisticated bistro look.

In a similar fashion, Katie uses Moroccan glazed terra-cotta tile, or zellige, hand cut in geometric patterns ranging from simple squares to eight-pointed stars, to form backsplashes that always exceed the role of back-of-the-counter protector. As she often says, "If you like the tile, run with it," all the way up to the ceiling. Instead of a truncated fragment or mere decorative strip, above-counter tile in Katie's kitchens acts as wallpaper—in more durable form. Though zellige tiles are often assembled in traditional complex patterns, Katie typically opts for a more tone-on-tone color scheme in a simple geometric. A small basketweave of blue and gray fills the under-cabinet space of a Connecticut kitchen (see pages 152 and 153). For a California kitchen, she chose a trellislike pattern of blue-green tiles mixed with grays and whites (see page 162). Not only do zellige tiles provide an endless array of patterns, but their semi-transparent glazed surfaces and the subtle irregularity of the overall mosaic produce clean, shimmering walls for kitchens. At the same time, they lend a handmade quality to the most machinelike room in the house.

The individual designs on square cement tiles form a larger pattern when they are assembled that can vary depending on how they are arranged or look entirely different in different color combinations.

TOP Lucifer cement tile in white, gray, and pale green.

BOTTOM Aureola in red and orange.

Wallpaper

BOOKS ARE AMONG KATIE'S FAVORITE RESOURCES, NOT ONLY for overall design inspiration but also for all kinds of decorative motifs. She always has a stack by her bedside and takes a large selection along when she relocates to the Massachusetts coast for the month of August. It's there that she works on her designs for the wallpaper collection she's been producing since 2009. She figures out imagery, scale, and color by hand, unaided by technology save for a copy machine that facilitates playing with scale. She and the screen maker later work out the repeat for the 27-inch-wide rolls of paper.

A book surveying classic Japanese motifs may yield a textile from which Katie extracts a border that then forms the basis for an overall pattern like that of her paper "Wave." In a book of eighteenth-century botanical etchings she may find a leaf or flower that blossoms, by change of line weight, color, and scale, into something utterly contemporary. She may detect a tiny motif in a miniature painting from India that, exploded in size, forms the basis of a dramatically abstract wallpaper.

Many of Katie's wallpapers project an exotic air because they are rooted in classical imagery of foreign lands. Elephants sidle up to a pagoda in her "Pagoda" paper. Pashas parade across her "Attendants" paper. Her best-selling paper, "Leaf," is filled with giant egg-shaped Mughal leaves. Other papers practically emit the ocean breezes that drift over Katie's worktable at the shore. Crabs skitter across a paper named for them, playing peekaboo in the seaweed, and in "Beetlecat," the New England wooden sailboat for which the paper is named cuts back and forth amid stylized waves.

TOP Bubbles in the form of dots rise from the sprays of fan-shaped forms in "Seaweed," in pink.

ABOVE Katie's "Attendants" wallpaper, here in purple, features men in traditional Turkish costume (balloon pants, turbans, shoes with upturned toes) weaving through pomegranates cut in half.

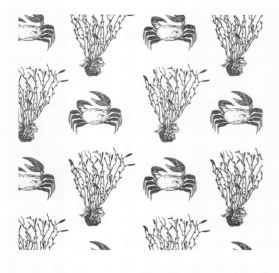 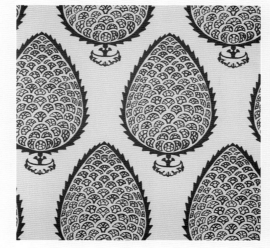 

 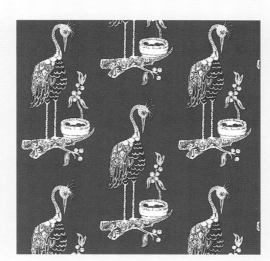 

TOP ROW, LEFT TO RIGHT
Crabs and seaweed alternate on "Crab," in orange on white; "Leaf," here in periwinkle, papers Katie's daughter's room (see pages 204–5); crescents accent medallions containing birds in "Oiseau," in red.

MIDDLE ROW, LEFT TO RIGHT
A slice of moon hangs over a pagoda flanked by elephants in "Pagoda," in persimmon; "Crane" features a repeat of the long-legged bird watching over a nest, in birch; a stylized spray of flowers is encircled by a crescent in "Moon Flower," in tangerine.

BOTTOM ROW, LEFT TO RIGHT
Squiggles that could be tendrils or sea spray erupt between layers of fish scales, or perhaps abstract wave forms, in "Wave"; the green colorway of "Seaweed"; wind fills the orange sails of a boat cutting through waves in "Beetlecat," in cream.

Sources

Alexander Cohane
28 East 73rd Street, 6D
New York, NY 10021
(646) 249-0867
www.alexandercohane.com
European antiques

Ann-Morris Antiques
239 East 60th Street
New York, NY 10022
(212) 755-3308
Lighting and furniture

Anthony Lawrence-Belfair
(TRADE ONLY)
53 West 23rd Street
New York, NY 10010
(212) 206-8820
www.anthonylawrence-belfair.com
Custom upholstery and curtains

Ashbury Hides
1232 S. La Cienega Blvd. #104
Los Angeles, CA 90035
(310) 360-1520
www.ashburyhides.com
Leather in a wide range of colors

Beauvais Carpets
595 Madison Avenue, 3rd Floor
New York, NY 10022
(212) 688-2265
www.beauvaiscarpets.com
Hand-woven carpets and antique rugs

Carlos de la Puente Antiques
241 East 60th Street
New York, NY 10022
(212) 751-2282
www.delapuenteantiques.com
Antique and vintage lighting

Charles H. Beckley
979 Third Avenue, Suite 911
New York, NY 10022
(212) 759-8450
www.chbeckley.com
Custom mattresses, box springs, and beds

Christopher Spitzmiller
248 West 35th Street
New York, NY 10001
(212) 563-1144
www.christopherspitzmiller.com
Handmade ceramic lamps

Chuck Hettinger Studio
208 East 13th Street, 1R
New York, NY 10003
(212) 614-9848
Hand-painted wall stencils

Cove Landing
995 Lexington Avenue
New York, NY 10021
(212) 288-7597
18th- and 19th-century English and Continental furniture and objects

David Melchior Cabinetry
Brooklyn Navy Yard
Building 275, Suite 204
Brooklyn, NY 11205
(718) 858-0832
Custom lacquer furniture

Doris Leslie Blau
306 East 61st Street, 7th floor
New York, NY 10065
(212) 586-5511
www.dorisleslieblau.com
Fine antique carpets

Durite Concepts
15 Cutter Mill Road
Great Neck, NY 11021
(516) 334-4533
www.durite.net
Custom tabletops, counters, and floors

Du Verre Hardware
(416) 593-0182
www.shopduverre.com
"Pomegranate" and other distinctive hardware

Elizabeth Eakins
654 Madison, Suite 1409
New York, NY 10065
(212) 628-1950
www.elizabetheakins.com
Natural fiber rugs and fabrics

Farrow & Ball
112 Mercer Street
New York, NY 10012
(212) 334-8330
http://us.farrow-ball.com/
Traditional paints

1st Dibs @ NYDC
200 Lexington Avenue, 10th Floor
New York, NY 10016
(646) 293-6633
www.1stdibs.com
Antiques and accessories

Fortuny
979 Third Avenue, Suite 1632
New York, NY 10022
(212) 753-7153
www.fortuny.com
Venetian fabrics

Fresco Decorative Painting
324 Lafayette Street, 5th Floor
New York, NY 10012
(212) 966-0676
frescodecorativepainting.com
Decorative wall finishers

Galerie Shabab
112 Madison Avenue
New York, NY 10016
(212) 725-5444
www.galerieshabab.com
Antique carpets

Gerald Bland
1262 Madison Avenue
New York, NY 10128
(212) 987-8505
www.geraldblandinc.com
Art and antiques

Harbinger
752 North La Cienega Blvd.
West Hollywood, CA 90069
(310) 858-6884
www.harbingerla.com
Fabric, furniture, and lighting

Holland & Sherry
979 Third Avenue, Suite 1402
New York, NY 10022
(212) 355-6241
www.hollandandsherry.com
Unique fabrics

James Sansum
33 East 68th Street, 6th Floor
New York, NY 10065
(212) 288-9455
www.jamessansum.com
Fine and decorative art and antiques

JM Upholstery (TRADE ONLY)
10-10 44th Avenue, 5th Floor
Long Island City, NY 11101
(718) 786-0104
www.jmupholsteryinc.com
Upholstery workroom

Johansen Interiors
706 No. Division Street
Peekskill, NY 10566
(914) 739-6293
Window treatments

John Nalewaja
170 West 74th Street
New York, NY 10023
(212) 496-6135
*Scenic wallpaper installation
and restoration*

John Rosselli Antiques
306 East 61st Street
New York, NY 10065
(212) 750-0060
www.johnrosselliantiques.com
Eclectic antiques

John Salibello Antiques
211 East 60th Street
New York, NY 10022
(212) 838-5767
www.johnsalibelloantiques.com
*Mid-20th-century furniture
and lighting*

Joseph Biunno
21-07 Borden Avenue, 3rd Floor
Long Island City, NY 10011
(718) 729-5630
Custom furniture maker

Karl Szadok
41 Peacock Lane
Levittown, NY 11756
(516) 984-6160
Leather wall and floor tile specialist

La Forge Française
100 Kroemer Avenue
Riverhead, NY 11901
(631) 591-0572
laforgefrancaise.com
*Metal furniture, accessories,
and ornaments*

Lars Bolander
232 East 59th Street, 3rd Floor
New York, NY 10022
(212) 924-1000
www.larsbolander.com
*Swedish and Continental furniture
and antiques*

Lee Calicchio
306 East 61st Street
New York, NY 10021
(212) 588-0841
www.leecalicchioltd.com
*18th-, 19th-, and 20th-century
furniture and lighting*

Leontine Linens
3806 Magazine Street
New Orleans, LA 70115
(504) 899-7833
www.leontinelinens.com
Custom bedding and linens

Marash Elezaj
One Creaville Lane
Crestwood, NY 10707
(914) 793-8678
Wall painter and wall covering installer

Mecox Gardens
962 Lexington Avenue
New York, NY 10021
(212) 249-5301
www.mecoxgardens.com
Garden furniture and accessories

Morgik Metal Designs
145 Hudson Street
New York, NY 10013
(212) 463-0304
www.morgik.com
*Metal curtain hardware, railings,
and furniture*

Mosaic House
62 West 22nd Street
New York, NY 10010
(212) 414-2525
www.mosaichse.com
Moroccan tile

Orange
8111 Beverly Blvd.
Los Angeles, CA 90048
(323) 782-6898
Fun lighting and antiques

Paul Lanier
1703 Castro Street
San Francisco, CA 94131
(415) 695-7970
Decorative sculptor

Penn & Fletcher (TRADE ONLY)
21-07 41st Avenue, 5th Floor
Long Island City, NY 11101
(212) 239-6868
www.pennandfletcher.com
Embroidery

Robert Abbey
(828) 322-3480
www.robertabbey.com
Corner sconces and other lighting

Ruzzetti & Gow
1015 Madison Avenue
New York, NY 10025
(212) 327-4281
www.ruzzettiandgow.com
Natural curiosities

Samuel & Sons
983 Third Avenue
New York, NY 10022
(212) 704-8000
www.samuelandsons.com
Tapes and trims

Secondhand Rose
230 Fifth Avenue, Suite 510
New York, NY 10001
(212) 393-9002
www.secondhandrose.com
Vintage wallpaper

Shades from the Midnight Sun
10 Wildway
Bronxville, NY 10708
(914) 779-7237
Unique and clever lampshades

Stark Carpet
979 Third Avenue, 11th Floor
New York, NY 10022
(212) 752-9000
www.starkcarpet.com
Carpets and rugs

Studio Four
900 Broadway, Suite 204
New York, NY 10003
(212) 475-4414
www.studiofournyc.com
Textiles and carpets

Style by Annick de Lorme
PO Box 1486
New York, NY 10276
(212) 219-0447
www.capsudusa.com
Bistro chairs and stools

Urban
545 West 45th Street, 3rd Floor
New York, NY 10036
(212) 664-0800
Custom lacquer linen tables

Vaughan
979 Third Avenue, Suite 1511
New York, NY 10022
(212) 319-7070
www.vaughandesigns.com
Lighting of all kinds

Virginia Di Sciascio
(TRADE ONLY)
19 East 71st Street
New York, NY 10021
(212) 794-8807
Antique textiles and pillows

Urban Electric Company
2130 N. Hobson Avenue
North Charleston, SC 29405
(843) 723-8140
www.urbanelectricco.com
Hand-crafted and bespoke lighting

Westtown Chandelier Restoration
74 County Route 12
Westtown, NY 10998
(845) 726-0929
Lighting doctors

ARCHITECTS

The following architects designed
the apartments and houses featured
in this book

Anik Pearson Architect
171 Madison Avenue
New York, NY 10016
House in Arkansas

Botticelli & Pohl Architects
82 Easton Street
Nantucket, MA 02554
House in Nantucket

John B. Murray Architect
48 West 37th Street
New York, NY 10018
Apartment on Park Avenue

MR Architecture + Decor
245 West 29th Street
New York, NY 10001
Apartment in New York: modern

Peter Pennoyer Architects
432 Park Avenue South
New York, NY 10016
• *Houses in California, Connecticut,
and Virginia*
• *Apartments in New York: East
River and Central Park*

Ron Czajka Architects
48 Young Avenue
Pelham, NY 10803
Apartment in New York: prewar

Acknowledgments

Until my client Mark Magowan, co-owner of Vendome Press, became my publisher by convincing me to do a book of my work, I had never seriously considered embarking on such a project. As my office can attest, we seemed busy enough designing and more than busy buttoning up details. So I am very grateful to Mark for his encouragement and support and also to his stellar team: Jackie Decter, our editor; Celia Fuller, who designed the book; and Heather MacIsaac, who wrote the text. The pictures make the book, and I am very lucky to have had the great talents of Eric Piasecki, along with Scott Frances, Bill Waldron, Lucas Allen, Pieter Estersohn, and the late Fernando Bengoechea.

To start at the beginning, I owe the most to my mother, Connie Ridder, who taught me by her example—raising a family, then becoming a lawyer—that hard work opens doors. I may not have inherited her level of perseverance but she has always cheered me on when I've flagged.

In my eight years of working for decorating magazines I had mentors who inspired me, including Carolyn Sollis, Lou Gropp, Anna Wintour, Greg Wakabayashi, and the late Sarah Kaltman Cantor at *House & Garden*, and Peggy Kennedy at *House Beautiful*. Being an editor allowed me to observe the best decorators in the business at work, to experience great rooms firsthand, and to work with talented photographers, learning the invaluable lessons that come with seeing rooms through the lens.

All of my projects are collaborations and I am especially grateful to the women in my office: Susannah Beams, Robin Henry Goldman, Nathalie Cort Schubert, and Olga Dykunets; and before them Shaun Jackson, Dalia Shaoul Benzaquen, Carrie Weinstein, Maria Pollard, Susan Lawson, Laurie Reynolds, and Remy Crisci. For any project, the bar is set by the architecture. I would like to thank Gregory Gilmartin, Tom Nugent, and Liz Graziolo, who are my husband's partners, as well as Jim Taylor and Anik Pearson, Ron Czajka, John Murray, MR Architecture + Decor, and Lisa Botticelli.

I am also thankful for the talent and professionalism of my vendors, including Joan Johansen, Anthony Lawrence-Belfair, JM Upholstery, Penn & Fletcher, Marash Elezaj,

Shades from the Midnight Sun, Chuck Hettinger, and Charles H. Beckley, Inc.

The book would not have been possible without my wonderful clients, who consistently take the leap of faith that commissioning a decorator requires. More than that, they generously allowed me to photograph their houses.

I am deeply indebted to the magazine editors who have given me the chance to put my work before the public; this is where decorating careers are made. Margaret Russell was an early and loyal supporter and friend. Anita Sarsidi, Sarah Medford, Pamela Fiori, Dara Caponigro, Penelope Green,

Marion McEvoy, and Anne Foxley all contributed their energy and vision—they are the kind of editors who teach us as they present our work.

Finally, I thank my family. Our children—Jane, Tony, and Gigi—have always encouraged me and watched, with bemusement yet patiently, the trial appearances of furniture in our house and ever-evolving color schemes. My husband, Peter Pennoyer, shares my passion for design. We have learned much together and from each other, in our collaborations and in our travels, but he has always encouraged me to express my own vision—even when it is more colorful than his.

Katie Ridder

First published in the United States of America in 2011 by
The Vendome Press
1334 York Avenue
New York, NY 10021
www.vendomepress.com

ISBN 978-0-86565-272-9

EDITOR: Jacqueline Decter
PRODUCTION EDITOR: Alecia Reddick
DESIGNER: Celia Fuller

Library of Congress Cataloging-in-Publication Data
MacIsaac, Heather Smith.
  Katie Ridder rooms / Heather Smith MacIsaac.
    p. cm.
  ISBN 978-0-86565-272-9
  1. Ridder, Katie--Themes, motives. 2. Interior decoration--United States.
I. Title.
  NK2004.3.R62A4 2011
  747--dc23
                                                    2011020584

Printed by Toppan Printing Co., Ltd., in China
Second printing

PHOTOGRAPHY CREDITS

All photos by Eric Piasecki, with the exception of the following:

Fernando Bengoechea, pp. 7, 15, 107, 135, 164, 165, 180 left

Scott Frances, pp. 8, 20, 21, 31, 50–51, 52–53, 73 right, 74–75, 76–77, 92–93, 111,
114–15, 124–25, 150–51, 154–55, 160, 171, 172, 173, 180–81, 200, 209

Luca Trovato, p. 12

Lucas Allen, pp. 16, 17, 18, 19, 38–39, 40, 42, 72–73, 90, 91, 102, 123, 126, 127, 129,
134, 156, 157, 158, 159, 161, 176 top left, 177, 179, 182, 183, 201, 202, 214, 219, 220, 231

Pieter Estersohn, pp. 22–23, 70–71, 114 left, 150 left

Trevor Tondro, p. 27

William Waldron, pp. 37, 44–45, 46, 47, 138–39, 167, 174, 175, 178, 212, 215,
224–25, front cover

Facundo Zuviría, pp. 80, 81, 82, 83

Jonathan Wallen, p. 221

Mosaic House, pp. 232, 233

Jay Ackerman, p. 239

PAGE 2 Behind a vintage crystal waterfall chandelier, Andreas
Gursky's photograph *Shanghai* gives extra dimension and dynamism
to a traditional New York dining room. The ice blue leather of the
dining chairs complements the yellow in the photograph.

PAGE 4 Cement tiles carpet a solarium in Arkansas that is
furnished with both airy and weighty furniture to provide year-
round comfort. Amid the cool blues and aquas, the red of the sofa
is an unexpected anchor of color.